Praise for *The Education of an Accidental CEO*

"David has always had the natural leadership gift of 'taking people with him,' but he never stopped learning, always valued others no matter what their background, and always stayed true to who he is. His great personal story provides lessons to anyone who has the privilege of leading. David makes working fun, and his passion is infectious. His rise to CEO was no accident!"

—Brenda Barnes, chairman and CEO
of the Sara Lee Corporation

"I'm a big fan of David Novak. I think he's one of the great CEOs in America. His story is full of gems that can help everyone look at their life and career in a different way. Read it!"

—Ken Blanchard, coauthor of
The One Minute Manager and *Leading at a Higher Level*

"An entertaining, humorous, honest, and inspiring message from an extraordinary person who engenders trust and instills self-confidence."

—Larry Bossidy, coauthor of
Execution and *Confronting Reality*

"If CEOs were selected like NFL quarterbacks, David Novak would be a first-round draft pick. I would certainly like to have him running a Berkshire company. After you read this book, you will know why."

—Warren Buffett

"*The Education of an Accidental CEO* is just plain fun to read and reminds me of all the things I still need to do better at JPMC. More important, though, is the message—no matter whether you are a CEO or just starting out—that each and every day provides the opportunity to learn and get better at what you do, because as David says 'you never know what you're capable of.' His book is smart with heart, and you'll see how far openness and honesty can get you. In short, very far."

—**Jamie Dimon,** chairman and CEO
of JPMorgan Chase

"David Novak is a great business leader and a wonderful guy. Our companies have very little in common, yet I have learned a lot from Dave. He is great with people, an innovator, and one of the best global thinkers I have met. This book is filled with the 'little things' that authentic leaders do every day to build a great business. The best leaders are the best learners. Dave's 'journey' brings the skill of learning to life."

—**Jeffrey R. Immelt,** chairman and CEO
of General Electric

"The best thing about this book is not that it's a nice story filled with simple wisdom—both of which are true. It's that its author, David Novak, is completely authentic and means every word of it. What a great lesson for anyone striving for real success."

—**Patrick Lencioni,** author of *The Five Dysfunctions of a Team* and president of the Table Group

"*The Education of an Accidental CEO* is a wonderful journey tracking the aspects of leadership. David Novak is the classic type-A personality who possesses the insatiable desire to improve and make those around him rise to new levels. Everyone is in search of the secret. This book has found it. A motivational must!"

—**Rick Pitino**

THE EDUCATION OF
AN ACCIDENTAL CEO

THE EDUCATION OF AN

ACCIDENTAL
CEO

LESSONS LEARNED FROM
THE TRAILER PARK
TO THE CORNER OFFICE

DAVID NOVAK
with *John Boswell*

CROWN
BUSINESS
NEW YORK

Published in the United States by Crown Business,
an imprint of the Crown Publishing Group,
a division of Random House, Inc., New York.
www.crownpublishing.com

Crown Business is a trademark and the Rising Sun
colophon is a registered trademark
of Random House, Inc.

Taking People with You is a registered
trademark of Yum! Brands, Inc.

Library of Congress Cataloging-in-Publication Data

Novak, David, 1953–
    The Education of an accidental CEO: lessons
learned from the trailer park to the corner office / by
David Novak with John Boswell. —1st ed.
        p. cm.

1. Novak, David.   2. Yum! Brands (Firm).
3. Restaurateurs—United States—Biography.
4. Success in business.   I. Title.

TX910.5.N68A3 2007
647.95092—dc22
[B]
                            2007017922

                    ISBN 978-0-307-39369-2

        Printed in the United States of America

            DESIGN BY LEONARD HENDERSON

            10 9 8 7 6 5 4 3 2 1

                    First Edition

To my wife, Wendy,
my best friend, my partner, and the love of my life

CONTENTS

THE EDUCATION OF
AN ACCIDENTAL CEO

INTRODUCTION

"You Never Know What You're Capable Of"

When I first said to my wife, Wendy, that I was thinking about writing a book, she asked me—partially in jest, I hope—why anyone would want to read a book about a CEO they had probably never heard of. That question stopped me in my tracks and got me thinking about what I have to say that might be useful to anyone.

As the CEO of Yum! Brands, the biggest restaurant company in the world and home to KFC, Taco Bell, Pizza Hut, Long John Silver's, and A&W All American Food, there are any number of extraordinary experiences that could have popped into my head. But what jumped out at me that day was a trip I took a few years back to Washington, D.C., for the opening of a KFC in one of D.C.'s toughest neighborhoods.

As I watched our team working together, I marveled at the motivation and the attitude that made the launch so successful. But that was nothing compared to the surprise visit I made to the same store seven months later. Sales were up, the atmosphere was full of energy, and the customer service

1

was as good or better than it had been on opening day. I asked a team member how she had managed to sustain so much positive energy in such a tough environment, and she said something that I'll never forget: "You know, you never know what you're capable of."

That one experience pretty much sums up my message in this book, and, to a large extent, my career. Fortunately, I never totally knew "what I was capable of " as I broke through barriers and rose up through the ranks to become CEO of a nearly one-million-employee company, Yum! Brands, at the age of forty-six.

While my rapid rise to the top might suggest that I had some master plan, brilliantly conceived and impeccably executed, nothing could be further from the truth. This is why I often describe my career as "accidental"—more a matter of the paths not taken than the paths that were—yet while always pushing the boundaries and taking advantage of opportunities that happened to come my way.

My early education was far from typical when you consider that I grew up in a series of trailer parks and was constantly moving around. Then, rather than major in business, I enrolled in the journalism school at the University of Missouri.

After graduation, the career "accidents" started to happen right away. I took a job as a $7,200-a-year advertising copywriter with ambitions of one day becoming a creative director. Instead, I became an account executive. I chose a career in advertising with the hopes of working for one of the big New York agencies. Instead, I ended up in Dallas, Texas. I took a job managing an account for Frito-Lay with the idea of learning the packaged-foods business.

Instead, I ended up working for Pizza Hut, which I liked so much I assumed I would spend the rest of my career in the restaurant business. But then I was offered the incredible experience of becoming head of marketing (and later the chief operating officer) of the beverage division of PepsiCo, one of the best-run companies in the world. Then almost out of nowhere, I was back in the restaurant business again, but this time as president of Pepsi-owned KFC and later of both KFC and Pizza Hut.

Finally, just as I began to consider myself a PepsiCo "lifer," I learned the restaurant division was going to be spun off and that I might have a shot at becoming the CEO of this new public company. Admittedly, this last move was no accident. In fact, in my aggressive pursuit of the position, I almost got myself fired, but that's a story for later in the book.

I guess you could say that while I didn't always know where I was going, I'm delighted at where I ended up. It's been an amazing journey and along the way I've had some extraordinary learning opportunities.

How many people, for instance, get to be coached by one of the world's top image consultants—one of his "other" clients was Johnny Carson—admittedly, for the purpose of adding a little polish? Or learn to overcome the jitters from a professional public speaking coach? How many people get to benefit from a little one-on-one guidance from the likes of Warren Buffett, Jack Welch, and John Wooden? Or get to visit some of the world's greatest companies to observe their best practices firsthand? Or have the opportunity to serve on the board of one of the world's biggest banks?

This is just the tip of the iceberg, but these are the kinds of experiences I have been lucky enough to have. By sharing with you what I've learned from them, maybe there is something that will help accelerate your own learning curve.

Because I never had a formal business education, a lot of what I've learned may also be unconventional and was often self-taught. Though I've had some amazing teachers (virtually every boss I've had went on to run a big company), I've also had to learn by doing and, more often than I'd like to admit, learn by failing. Failure is a great teacher and I have been its student on more than one occasion.

Do you, for instance, remember Crystal Pepsi, the "clear Pepsi"? It was my idea during my stint as head of marketing for Pepsi and it was supposed to be my career maker, my big new product breakthrough. That didn't happen. In fact *Time* magazine called it one of the worst new product ideas of the twentieth century. But it did lead to a better understanding of the importance of listening, especially when people are trying to warn me that I'm about to drive off a cliff. (I still think Crystal Pepsi would have worked if I'd only been more open to criticism, but I guess we'll never know.)

While PepsiCo served as my business school, when Yum! Brands was spun off on October 7, 1997, I got the once-in-a-lifetime opportunity to create a new culture from scratch, to lead others in building a public company, and to travel the world as we turned Yum! Brands into a global powerhouse.

Perhaps the one thing I am most proud of is that we are now benchmarked by other companies for what we do in terms of rewarding and recognizing our own people. In the photograph on the back cover of this book I am holding some of my recognition awards and, as you can see, I try to add an element of fun to go along with a monetary award. In fact, I very much believe that creating a sense of fun and keeping up everyone's energy level is part of my job description.

I also got the opportunity to start giving back, to begin to share what I had learned with others. This is when I first began to teach a leadership program of my own devising called Taking People with You to a wide variety of people at Yum! Brands, from first-time supervisors to senior executives. I have now given this seminar almost fifty times to approximately 2,500 of our employees.

What I have discovered as a result is how much I love to teach. In many ways I see myself as the Everyman CEO, and frankly, this stuff isn't rocket science. But because I've experienced it firsthand, I believe that legitimacy makes people want to learn and listen. Of course, that's the other half of the equation. If people aren't listening to what you have to share, then it's not teaching; it's babbling.

I feel incredibly blessed and energized to have been given the opportunity I now have. I also feel the awesome responsibility. I am presiding over one of the great experiments in business: finding ways to motivate and inspire a team of almost a million people spread around the world while keeping them moving ahead and rowing in the same direction.

What I want to do most of all with this book is to help people realize their ambitions, no matter what direction their careers may take them, by showing, up close and personal, how I've been able to realize my own. The part I like best about the leadership program I teach at Yum! is that magical moment at the end of the day when everyone gets together in little informal groups and talks about what they've learned. That's really emotional for me. It's like I've made a difference in their lives. If I can do the same for you with this book, then it will be all I hoped it could be.

The Spin-off

Taking an Unexpected Shot at the Top

I guess when you change trailer parks thirty-two times and live in twenty-three states by the time you're in seventh grade, you learn how to make the most out of new situations, even those that turn your life upside down. PepsiCo's decision ten years ago to spin off its restaurant group and create a new public company was one of those times for me. It had been a closely guarded secret; when Roger Enrico, PepsiCo's chairman and CEO, called me into his office to tell me the news, I hadn't had a clue—and I was head of both KFC and Pizza Hut, two of the three restaurant chains that were being spun off.

I understood why they were doing it. At the time PepsiCo was something of a two-headed beast, with its restaurants—KFC, Pizza Hut, and Taco Bell—on one side and its packaged-goods brands, Pepsi and Frito-Lay, on the other. Wall Street analysts had been talking for some time about the restaurants being a drag on earnings. The thinking was that PepsiCo would do better in the eyes of investors if it shed what was perceived as "dead weight."

Rather than sell its restaurant chains outright, PepsiCo

formed a new company dedicated solely to the restaurant business, which it hoped would give each of the individual restaurant companies a better chance to thrive. Of course the big question then was "Who's going to run it?"

Honestly, until that point, the thought of being CEO of a public company had never entered my mind. I loved being part of PepsiCo and had never even interviewed anywhere else during my eleven years working in its different divisions. I saw myself as a Pepsi lifer, and besides, as president of Pizza Hut and KFC, I already had my hands full with more challenges than I even wanted.

Nevertheless, I've always believed in jumping on opportunities when they come my way, and opportunity was clearly knocking loudly at my door. As soon as I started to think about it, I immediately assumed that I would be chosen to head up this new entity. I had already proven myself by turning around KFC, which had been struggling before I became president, and I was on my way to doing the same with Pizza Hut.

But when Roger called me up to talk about it, he told me that I was going to be the "coleader." Apparently he and others felt that I didn't know enough about the financial side of the business to be effective at doing the Wall Street dance, which, admittedly, was going to be very important to a new company.

My partner in this new enterprise was to be John Antioco, then the head of Taco Bell. He had joined the company a year earlier and was starting to make some progress turning Taco Bell around. But even more important to Roger was that he had previously helped take the convenience-store chain Circle K out of Chapter 11, so he knew his way around the financial community.

Basically, Roger had two guys he didn't want to lose in the spin-off, me and John, so his solution was to team us up. When I asked him what he meant by "running the company together," he told me: "John will be the chairman and CEO, and you will be the president. John will be Mr. Outside and you'll be Mr. Inside, the spiritual leader of the company."

Being a "spiritual leader" is what I had become known for at PepsiCo. Roger thought of me as someone who had a special talent for firing up an organization and making its people feel valued, because that's what I had done in all my leadership positions. I knew how to get through to people, how to set a vision for a company and rally the troops around it, but it's not all I knew how to do. I was glad that Roger had such faith in me, but at the same time, the idea of being just president, and number two to someone who had less restaurant experience than I, didn't sit too well with me. Still, a couple days later I met John Antioco for dinner, figuring I owed it to Roger and the company to give the idea a chance.

John and I talked for a few hours, and we got on pretty well. But, as he told me about his background, I couldn't help but think that if he was qualified to be CEO, then I was too. He had a background in marketing and operations, and so did I. I liked him and he was a nice guy, an accomplished guy, but, I thought, so was I.

As for financial expertise, it didn't sound to me like John knew all that much more than I did. Besides, I figured, I've always been a learner. When I moved from executive vice president of sales and marketing to chief operating officer at the Pepsi-Cola Company, I hardly knew anything about operations, but I had learned. When I became president of KFC, I had never before been the top guy, but I quickly got myself up to speed. Now there was a new aspect of business that I needed to master in order to keep moving forward, and I was confident I could not only do it but do it well.

As I walked out of the restaurant that night, I flashed back to my upbringing in a series of trailer parks and the challenges that had meant for me. With my family constantly moving around during my early childhood, I was always the new kid on the block, always having to prove myself. I also thought about how often my lack of an MBA had threatened to hold me back but how I had persevered anyway to become one of the youngest division heads in PepsiCo's history. I realized then that my feelings had nothing to do with John and everything to do with me. He was a talented, capable person (he ended up becoming the chairman and CEO of Blockbuster), but the truth was, I wanted that job and there was no doubt in my mind that if it was between me and him, then I deserved it.

I returned to Roger's office later that week to tell him what I thought. "You don't know what you don't know," he told me when I said I wanted to run the company myself. What he meant was, I may not have been able to see my own shortcomings clearly, but he could.

Roger is brilliant, a great leader, and I respect his opinion immensely. He's also one of the most tough-minded CEOs in the annals of American business. I knew it would be hard to change his mind, but I remember thinking to myself, "I've worked too hard and I've come too far to back off now. I'm not about to take a backseat to someone who is no more qualified than me."

As it turned out, I did have to share the reins of the new company, but with someone other than John and only for a short period of time. After almost getting fired for trying to go around Roger's decision, I had to swallow my pride and make amends with him. Then we came up with a compromise. I agreed to be vice chairman and president for three years with the understanding that, assuming I had earned the right, I would then take over the top position. (Obviously, there are no real guarantees in business unless you own the joint.)

I also got to suggest who would be my CEO for those first three years, although the decision was solely Roger's. His name was Andy Pearson, and I had a tremendous amount of respect for him. Andy, an acknowledged business guru and former president of PepsiCo, was a principal at Clayton, Dubilier & Rice, a top leveraged-buyout firm, when Roger recruited him to be our chairman and CEO. One of the first things Andy said to me was "You're going to report to me and everyone else is going to report to you." That suited me just fine.

Suddenly I was getting the chance to help create an entirely new public company where I could test all my theories about inspiring people and taking them on the ride of their lives. It was simply a matter of seeing how I could replicate the success I'd had at KFC, only this time on a much bigger stage.

In those days, I drew many times on the lessons of my humble upbringing, which is when I learned the difference between confidence and arrogance. That was going to come in handy now because I knew this was the chance of a lifetime, but I also knew it would be an incredible amount of work to get the new company to a place where it matched the vision in my head. There would surely be a lot of stumbling along the way. Still, I couldn't wait to get started.

2

Trailer Park Days

Being the New Kid
on the Block

My rise to the top may have been lightning quick—
I was only forty-six when I became CEO of Yum!
Brands in 2000—but the path has been anything
but direct. Who would have thought that a kid from the
trailer parks, whose childhood can best be described as no-
madic, would ever even have a chance at something like
that? Certainly I wouldn't have. In fact, like just about any
other kid, if you had asked me when I was young what I
wanted to be when I grew up, I would have told you that I
wanted to be a baseball player or a teacher, maybe follow in
the footsteps of my dad, Charles, who was a surveyor for
the government—anything but what I am today.

I'm proof positive that you never know what you're
capable of. Even though I had no idea when I was young
where I would end up, I think I had pretty good instincts
for which directions in life weren't for me. One of my
earliest memories is bringing home my report card in
grade school and watching my mom, Jean, open it. "This
is a good report card, David," she said, "but you got a C in
science."

13

I remember saying to my mom, "Gee, I guess this means I'm not going to be a scientist." I knew even then that whatever I was going to be one day, I definitely didn't want to be just average at it.

Moving as often as we did meant there was a high likelihood that either your family was one step ahead of the law or that your dad worked for the U.S. Coast and Geodetic Survey. Fortunately, in my case, it was the latter. My dad's job was to mark latitudes and longitudes for the nation's mapmakers, so every three or four months we'd pack up our gear and move on to the next location.

If anyone should have a sense of what heartland America is all about, it's me. Among the places I've lived are Gorham, New Hampshire; Ottumwa, Iowa; Dodge City, Kansas; Kenner, Louisiana; Marquette, Michigan; Crookston and Litchfield, Minnesota; Meadville and Knob Noster, Missouri; Batesville, Mississippi; Kimball, Nebraska; Tucumcari and Taos, New Mexico; Ahoskie, North Carolina; Zanesville, Ohio; Kittanning, Pennsylvania; Crescent, Oregon; Beeville, Abilene, and Freeport, Texas; Fairfax, Virginia; Oklahoma City, Oklahoma; Belle Fourche, South Dakota; Fargo, North Dakota; Elkins, West Virginia; and West Helena, Arkansas.

Support Is Everything

The words "trailer park" conjure up all sorts of negative stereotypes—of poverty and ignorance, of kids in ratty clothing and weeds growing out through the trailer wheels, of vast wastelands occasionally leveled by a tornado. These images have nothing to do with the reality of my childhood. In fact, in many ways, I can't imagine having had a more idyllic upbringing.

We were one of fifteen families on the survey team. Every time the team moved, we'd all pack up the government trucks with the trailers hitched to the back and head to the next trailer park. It was like a circus caravan without the elephants. There was always this great sense of anticipation—of new terrain to explore, of a new lake or stream to swim or fish in. The moving was always a game of who would get there first and get the best spot at the new trailer park. You took your neighborhood with you, which provided a strong infrastructure of support. When I played baseball, for example—and I was a pretty good athlete back then (I want to emphasize *back then*)—there would be about twenty people, extended-family members, watching my game. Everyone else on the team was lucky to get both their parents there, and I'd have a whole cheering section.

There were about thirty to forty kids in all. What's interesting, and what says a lot about the character of these families, is that I don't think any of the parents had college degrees but all of the kids in the survey party ended up going to college. We were a group that was pursuing the American Dream.

Trailer park living also makes for a close-knit family unit, mainly because you have no choice but to stick together. Kids today, with their computers and iPods and TVs, can disappear into their rooms and barely see their family. My TV watching was usually done with my parents, my two sisters, Susan and Karen, and me all clumped together on the couch in front of the one TV in our eight-by-forty-foot trailer. Deciding what shows to watch was one of my first lessons in negotiation and compromise. That's how I learned to love *The Ed Sullivan Show,* the Sunday-evening variety show that introduced Elvis Presley and the Beatles to a mainstream audience.

It's Never Too Early to Find a Mentor

Of course, there were obvious drawbacks to moving around every few months. My mother was very concerned about what it was doing to my education, but one day my favorite teacher during those years, Mrs. Anschultz, told her, "David is not even out of the fourth grade and he has already lived more places than most of these kids will visit in their lifetimes. Your son is getting an incredible education." My mom felt much better after that.

My dad has always been tremendously supportive, and he worked his tail off to give us a better life. But in many ways my mother was my first mentor. Every time we got to a new place, she would take me to the local school to get me registered and then say to me, "Look, David, you've got to take the initiative to make friends. Don't hang back and wait for the other kids to come to you. We're only going to be here for a few months, so make them count."

That's how I learned how to size people up in a hurry and how to figure out quickly who the good ones were and who I should avoid. As a result, when it comes to assessing people I've got a good gut instinct that I still listen to whenever I meet someone new (which, when you're a

CEO, is practically all the time) or have to decide whether to hire or promote someone.

Fear Is a Fact of Life

Going in cold to a new school every few months wasn't always a snap. There was a lot of anxiety involved, but I learned how to walk right through the anxiety and fear.

Fears are almost always about the future, even if it's the very near future, and I feared rejection as the new kid on the block. It's been my experience that 90 percent of the things we fear never happen and the other 10 percent don't happen the way we envision. But that doesn't make fear any less real. So while you're never going to make fear completely disappear, I've found that you can train yourself to conquer it.

Obviously we all have to deal with anxieties, both founded and unfounded, but the real enemy isn't anxiety; it's the indecision it can cause, which can lead to paralysis. As CEO of a very large company, I have to deal with my own anxieties every day. I'm constantly meeting new people, walking into new situations, and dealing with unforeseen problems. The more you learn to walk through it, the easier it gets.

Soon after becoming CEO of Yum! Brands, I went to my first meeting of the Business Council. Its members are one hundred twenty-five of the top CEOs in the country, and I was meeting these captains of industry for the first time. They are the people who run General Electric, Boeing, and General Motors, and they had no idea who I was. It wasn't all that different from a first day at a new school.

I quickly sized everyone up and, remembering that they all put their pants on the same way every morning, worked my way around the room. If it hadn't been for those early school experiences, I'm not sure this would have come so naturally to me in my later life.

I also learned that first impressions really matter. Anyone going into a new situation feels nervous or anxious. Whenever we moved someplace new, the first person to acknowledge me in some way made all the difference in the world. Jeff Immelt, the CEO of General Electric, was the first person at the Business Council meeting to walk up and introduce himself to me. He's head of one of the most respected companies in the world, so he didn't have to do that, but he made a point of doing it anyway. I remember being immediately impressed by the gesture and thinking, "It's no accident that he has his job."

Do the Right Thing

I was fortunate to grow up in an environment where good values were reinforced every day. When I was a kid, for example, I loved to play army, and one of my favorite Christmas presents one year was a canteen. I used it all the time—until I lost the lid. I was really upset about it until I magically found it a couple of weeks later when my mom and I were shopping at the store where she bought the canteen. After that, my mom noticed that I had the lid again and asked me where I'd found it. I couldn't lie to her, and when I told her I'd taken it from the store, she promptly took me by the hand, marched me back there, and made me apologize to the manager and return the lid. I learned that day that shoplifting should not be my vocation, and, more important, that it's never too late to do the right thing. Everyone makes mistakes and everyone has bad days, even the CEO, and I remember that lesson today when I cut someone off in a meeting or don't listen to someone's ideas. You can always go back and say you're sorry and then listen to what that person has to say.

Whether you're in heartland America or the middle of Borneo, most people know what good values are. A lot of us like to make a big show of our differences, but I believe that at our core, we are all pretty much the same. Running a company that has nearly a million employees spread over 112 countries around the world has reinforced that idea for me, but it's something that I actually learned a long time ago. There's not one set of good values for one person and another set for someone else. There's also not one set of good values for today and a whole new set of good values for next week. Good values are eternal.

I played a lot of sports growing up, and I learned many of my best lessons on fields and courts throughout the country. My dad managed my baseball team in Kimball, Nebraska, and he took a lot of pride in the job. We won the championship, but that's not what mattered most to him. He loved teaching kids, especially the ones who weren't that good, because helping them improve gave him tremendous satisfaction. I could go out and hit three home runs and then when we got home, he'd say, "Good job, David, but what happened with that one ball you let creep between your legs in the second inning?"

My dad always said things like that in a good-natured

way, but at the same time, he was really good at giving me the needle. He liked to have fun but he also knew how to raise the bar and to help make people better. Since the apple doesn't fall far from the tree, I do the same thing with my team members today. I always try to acknowledge what someone's done well before talking about what could be done better. Just recently, I tasted some new breakfast products for one of our restaurant brands that had taken forever to develop. I said, "Wow, these products are great, but will our customers get to eat them in my lifetime?" I believe in motivating with humor, so I said it not in a sarcastic way but in a way that made the team laugh. I was able to compliment their progress while also challenging them to step up the pace in bringing those products to the market.

Stereotypes Are Poison

Many people would look at the fact that I grew up in trailer parks and assume I must have had a disadvantaged youth, exactly the opposite of how it was. And I'm sure that my being a trailer park kid contributes to my sensitivity about negative stereotyping.

I remember that the town we lived in in Arkansas had segregated drinking fountains and how uncomfortable that made me feel because it was so different from other places I'd lived. I also remember being on the receiving end of people's prejudice. In New Mexico, we lived in a tough neighborhood where any newcomer was considered an enemy. Even my short walk home from school became a battle; these same two kids came after me every day before they even knew my name. My dad was the first one to tell me that there are just some things that shouldn't be tolerated. I came home crying one day and told him what had happened, and he said, "Well, you're going to have to go back out there and kick their butts."

"But, Dad, there are two of them," I protested.

He said, "Well, kick both their butts!"

I hate stereotyping of all sorts. It's just another form of prejudice, which I hate even more. When I go out to look at our restaurants, there are a lot of people out there doing everyday jobs who are just as smart as I am but maybe haven't had the same opportunities. But because they happen to be washing dishes or working the drive-thru people automatically assume that they don't have much to say that's worth listening to. That's a big mistake. Back when we launched our oven-roasted chicken pieces at KFC, for example, everyone at our corporate office thought the product was just great as it was. But then I talked to the cooks at a couple of our restaurants who showed me how difficult it was to make the product with consistent results in the real world. That insight sent us back to the drawing board. Thanks to those cooks, we found a quicker and simpler process for making the product, which saved us a ton of time and money in the long run.

In a business context, stereotyping absolutely destroys effective communication. You go in with some preconceived notion of who someone is or where someone is coming from, and you have almost no chance of really hearing what that person has to say. I had this problem with a high-profile ad agency I worked with at Pizza Hut. The agency is known for its creativity, but the people working on our account, and especially the head of the agency, were so afraid that we wouldn't get their ideas, they never listened to us. I ended up having to fire them because the communication between us was so bad. They couldn't get past their idea of us as just a bunch of guys in suits who couldn't possibly understand their perspective.

So much of what I learned during my unusual childhood would serve me well later on and continues to serve me in my role as a CEO. In fact, it probably would have served me well no matter where I ended up or what I ended up doing.

3

Little Fish, Big Pond

Breaking Through the Clutter

Have you ever felt like you were nothing but a cog in the machine, like you were just one of many? Me too.

When I was in sixth grade, my dad got promoted and we moved to Kansas City, our first "permanent" location. At first we lived in the Heart of America trailer court, the first big-city trailer park I'd ever been in. It was my best year yet and the first time I got to stay in one place for the entire year. I was popular in school and was even voted Most Likely to Succeed. It was also the last year I would live in a trailer court. After that we moved into a house—where we would remain throughout my junior high and high school years. I remember my mom and dad counting out their government bonds to make the down payment.

Our new home was a three bedroom split-level, and I got to have my own room, which was bigger than the entire living room of our trailer. The next year, however, I would get the awakening of my life.

When I started junior high, I went from a school with about fifty people in my class to one with about five hundred. The kids had their cliques, and I wasn't in any of them. I had always had an advantage when I was the new kid in school—it made me unique—but now I was just like everyone else. On top of that, I stopped growing. I had always been tall for my age, but starting in seventh grade, my growth leveled off and I went from being a star athlete to not even making the basketball team. I learned fast that there was a bigger, more competitive world out there and that there would always be someone better than me at something. It is a lesson I've learned and relearned many times since.

Play to Your Strength

The realization that I wasn't the best player on the team anymore actually helped open the world up for me. I started looking for other things that I was good at. In high school I discovered I was a good writer, so I became the editor of the school newspaper. I had a very supportive teacher, Mr. Harp, who told me I was good enough to write for the *New York Times* someday and that I could make $100,000 a year. Back then that seemed like more money than I could ever imagine.

Being newspaper editor was probably my first en-counter with the concept of "breaking through the clutter." Today, probably a day doesn't go by in which I don't make some business reference to that idea. I'm surprised none of our managers has ever said to me, "David, why don't you give that 'breaking through-the-clutter' thing a rest."

Why do I think this is so important? Because most business is white noise. Everything sort of blends together into a kind of dull hum. Whether it's your advertising, or trying to get a message through twenty layers of management, or making people understand the numbers, you've got to find a way to stand out. In some ways it's the first rule of communications. If your message is not getting heard, then it doesn't much matter what it is.

The "clutter" problem with high school newspapers is that they're all exactly the same. Because they are so limited by what they can cover and how, they are invariably boring. I decided to shake things up a bit.

We had a very good basketball team, one of the best in the state, but we were never able to win our conference. Somehow we'd always find a way to lose our big game. Our talent was great, so I figured it had to be the coaching.

I wrote an editorial about it. It wasn't nasty or mean-spirited, but I told it the way I saw it. The coach never molded our players into a team that played together well enough to win when it really counted. Well, that didn't go down so well. You simply weren't supposed to criticize any member of the faculty no matter what the circumstances. I almost got kicked out of school, but it got people's attention.

Breaking through the clutter is such a powerful concept that even when it's done badly it can still work. Once I graduated from college I needed a job quickly. I was applying to advertising agencies, so rather than send out a typical one-page résumé, I made up this dinky little brochure. It had my picture on the front, and on the back a little poem I had written about why someone should hire me. Recently

I looked for a copy with the idea that maybe I should reproduce it in this book. Fortunately, I couldn't find it because I'm sure it would make me cringe today. But it worked! I got a number of inquiries—and a job offer from my first real boss, Jim Walczy.

The First Rule of Advancement: Love What You Do

I had a bunch of odd jobs in high school—mowing lawns, construction, I was even a janitor for a summer. None of them paid particularly well, so when I saw an ad saying you could make seventy-five dollars a day selling, I went to downtown Kansas City and applied right away.

The ad was kind of vague—it didn't say what exactly you'd be selling—but the man I met impressed me right away. He wore a three-piece suit with a hankie in his pocket, and he drove a Lincoln Continental. He also made sure to flash me his big money clip full of bills. He was showing me the dream, and I bought into it. To me, this guy looked big-time.

The job, I finally found out, was going door-to-door selling encyclopedias. Someone would drop me off in the middle of a nearby town and then pick me up at the end of the day; it was up to me to start knocking on doors and make something happen.

The first time I went out I sold two sets of encyclopedias, which was a pretty good start, but I realized right away that I didn't feel so good about the accomplishment. The problem was, I was selling them to people who didn't need them. I sold one to this little old lady who didn't have any kids but was just happy to have someone to talk to for a while. I think she bought the books to thank me for spending time with her. The next day I sold another set, and in two days, I had made $225, which for me was a lot of money.

On the third day, I quit. It felt too much like I was hustling people. It just didn't feel right. I found out I was pretty good at selling but that I have to believe in what I sell.

Not long after that I left home to go to college. I chose to go to journalism school at the University of Missouri for two reasons. First, thanks to my time at the school paper, I had discovered that I liked writing, thought I was pretty good at it, and might even be able to earn a living doing it. Second, Missouri, with its in-state tuition, was one of the few places where I could afford to go.

The first couple of years I was really a bad student—I did way too much partying—but that started to change when I took an advertising course in my junior year. I liked the whole idea of influencing perceptions and changing and reinforcing behavior. I would watch TV commercials and try to deconstruct them—figure out what the advertiser was trying to do and whether or not he succeeded. What I was discovering is that I was turned on by advertising.

The importance of loving what you do is one of the oldest clichés in the book, but I believe it's essential to getting ahead, so much so that if you don't really like what you're doing, then you need to keep looking. My sister Susan decided in her late forties that she was burnt out on her job as division controller for a nursing-home company. She dreamed of owning her own clothing boutique, so one day she got up the courage to quit her job and follow her passion. Now she operates her own store, called Sisters, and she can't wait to go to work every day. The business has its challenges, but she's happier than she's ever been. She told me her only regret is that she didn't do it sooner. Life's too short not to do what you love if you get the chance. Besides, you never know what you're capable of until you give it a shot.

How do you know when you've hit on something that you may grow to love? In my case, reading David Ogilvy's *Confessions of an Advertising Man* really excited me. I still remember many of the stories, but more important, up to that point, the only nonfiction books I had read—other than biographies of baseball players like Jackie Robinson, Babe Ruth, and Mickey Mantle, which I voraciously consumed back then—were those assigned for a class. This was the first business book I actually chose to read on my own.

I love my job today because I still love marketing and advertising, I love people, and I love food. Our company spends almost two billion dollars a year on marketing, so I get to spend a lot of time on that. With almost one million employees around the world, I have plenty of opportunities to be with and affect different kinds of people. And I love our food. I eat at each of our restaurants almost every week, and I love going into our test kitchens to try out new things. All this means I get to spend time doing what I love every day. And just like everyone else, I'm simply better at the things I like doing. It's common sense, really, but the problem with common sense is that it's not all that common.

Get Right-Sized

In college I was elected rush chairman of my fraternity, and I discovered that I really liked recruiting, which is something that has served me well throughout my career. I would start off by asking my fellow students who were the best and brightest kids coming out of their former high schools. I loved the challenge of going after those people. Rather than wait for prospective pledges to come to campus, I'd go visit them in their homes. Then I would meet with their parents and, later, take their kid out to have a good time. We got one of the best pledge classes we'd ever had when I was rush chairman. Because I thought we had the best fraternity, I loved what I was selling and I was very aggressive about it.

After my success as rush chairman, I decided to run for president of the fraternity. I figured I was a shoo-in, but I lost. I was devastated but some of my friends helped me figure out where I'd gone wrong. I had become too cocky, arrogant. There were people who not only didn't vote for me but who were rooting for me to lose. This was hard to hear, but I think when you don't get what you want, you have to look in the mirror and ask yourself why. What I learned from this is the importance of staying "right-sized"—not thinking your you-know-what doesn't stink, and alternatively never getting too down on yourself.

College is where I met my best friend and my most trusted business advisor, my wife, Wendy. She has a great bull detector and really helps me keep things in perspective. Wendy has a very delicate way of letting me know when I'm getting out of line by saying things like "Get your ego in check" and "You're not the CEO around here." Without her, I never would have made it this far. It's funny to look back now and realize how easily I could have let her get away.

When Wendy and I first met, I thought she was the most beautiful girl on campus. I had worshipped her from afar since my freshman year, but I thought there was no way she would go out with me. Besides, I had heard that she only dated older guys. During my senior year I mentioned to a friend, who happened to be dating Wendy's roommate, that I had always had a crush on her but that I didn't think she would be interested in me. A few weeks before graduation I was at a bar with a group of my friends, and Wendy was down at the other end of the bar with a group of her friends. Across the entire length of the bar, she yelled at me, "Hey, Novak, when are you going to have enough guts to ask me out?"

We were married less than a year later.

4

Climbing Up and
Staying Grounded

Getting Down to Business

tarting my career was like experiencing the sense of
inadequacy I had felt back in junior high school all
over again. I was anxious, clueless, and didn't know
how I would ever fit in. I had made a commitment to get
into advertising, but almost no advertising agencies had
come to our campus to recruit.

I interviewed with a few companies that did come to
the University of Missouri, and it looked like I might get a
sales job at Procter & Gamble. I didn't, and that was probably a lucky break. As good a company as P&G is, it places
such a high premium on MBAs, I probably wouldn't have
been able to climb very high up its corporate ladder without going back to school. I probably would have been
thrown into a corporate maze, and who knows where I
would have ended up.

After I graduated from college in 1974, my primary
goal was to spend as much time with Wendy as possible.
She had plans to go away to Europe for the summer, and I
wanted to see her as often as I could before then. Right
before she left—and this was only about eight weeks after

we started dating—I asked her to marry me. To my surprise and delight, she said yes; then she promptly left the country. We planned to get married as soon as she returned, but I didn't have a penny to my name at that point. All of a sudden, I really needed a job.

A lot of kids know what they want to do and are well on their way to doing it before they graduate from college, but I wasn't one of them. My big plan was to move back home with my parents, find the best job I could, and make enough money to buy Wendy an engagement ring.

My parents were living in Maryland at the time, so most of the places where I applied for jobs were in the Washington, D.C., area. As I mentioned earlier, I sent out my dopey brochure/résumé and ended up getting a job working for Jim Walczy at a D.C. ad agency called R. Joseph Harrill & Farr. I started out as a copywriter making $7,200 a year, which doesn't sound like much, but it didn't matter because it was a perfect way to cut my teeth. Jim was a great first boss. He was quiet and subtle, but he always found a way to let me know that he thought I was doing a great job.

We were a tiny agency and all our accounts were local businesses—real estate brokers, community banks, et cetera. My first office was a little desk in the back corner with a big poster of a hamburger hanging on the wall behind it. I don't know why the hamburger was there, and I had no clue at the time that I'd end up in the restaurant business, but I now see it as a sign of things to come.

Working there was a great experience because I always had to start out with a blank sheet of paper. Jim would assign me an account and then just let me loose, so I learned by doing. There was really no one to turn to but myself. I had to think about the consumers and come up with my own ideas about how to reach them. One of my first assignments was a print campaign for the Bank of Bethesda. I put together a collage of old photos of people who had once worked for the bank. My tagline was: "These men worked hard for the day we could offer you free checking." People really liked it, and I started to realize that I could do this and do it well. That's when I learned how to put myself in the shoes of the customer, which has proved invaluable throughout my career.

Everything's Relative

Since Harrill & Farr was a small place, I worked with everyone in the company at one time or another. That really gave me a chance to watch people and decide who I wanted to be like and who I didn't want to be at all. I worked with a lot of creative people and spent a lot of time with our art director, but at the end of the day, I decided what I really wanted to be was one of the guys wearing the suits. I admired the account executives who worked with the clients and made the real money.

The one thing I've known about myself from early on is that I'm extremely competitive, and I would have been like that no matter where I ended up. Once you get into business, everything becomes relative. Whatever position you're in, you always take a look at your peers and decide whether they're better than you or not. Then, if you're competitive like me, you work to become better than them. Once you are, then you look at your boss and think, "Does he have something I don't have?" Then you work to become better than him, too. That's how my career has always worked.

One of the stories that David Ogilvy tells in his book is about one of the many jobs he had before he got into advertising. He was a cook at an upscale restaurant where the specialty of the house was the soufflé. As he told it, there was this one guy in the kitchen who kept messing up the soufflés. Finally one day, after he'd done it again, the head chef came in and fired him on the spot. Ogilvy wrote that he'd never forget how ruthless he thought that chef was at the time, but that that night, everyone was proud to be in the kitchen. Every time the soufflé maker failed, it had demoralized everyone else. They'd just think to themselves, "I'm better than him, but it doesn't seem to matter." His being fired was the best thing that could have happened to the kitchen staff because it meant that being better than someone else did matter.

Reward a Job Well Done

To make ends meet I also took a night job working the desk at the local Holiday Inn, which was my first real experience with customer service. This is where I learned not only the power of "service with a smile" but, as the lone night clerk, how to use my personality to calm down irate customers.

It's also where I first learned what it feels like to go unappreciated. One time the pop singer Engelbert Humperdinck checked in, along with his huge entourage. He was a very big entertainer at the time, and for a kid from the Midwest like myself, he might as well have been Elvis Presley. I gave them the best service imaginable, but when they checked out, they stiffed me on the tip. I'll remember until the day I die how bad that made me feel. It was probably my first realization about why rewarding people for a job well done is so important.

Today, rewarding and recognizing deserving employees is one of the cornerstones of my leadership philosophy. It has also contributed mightily to the success of our business by helping to keep our people motivated and excited to come into work every day. It also helps create an atmosphere of fun, and as I said before, people who enjoy their work always do a much better job than those who don't. So if you are out there, Engelbert Humperdinck (or whoever in your entourage was supposed to give me a tip), and you happen to read this, I want to personally thank you for being such a cheapskate.

Follow the Power

After about two years as a copywriter at Harrill & Farr, I felt I needed experience at a bigger agency, so I sent out letters to the top twenty-five ad agencies in the country. Wendy and I were married by then, and we had decided we were ready to move somewhere new. We pictured ourselves starting a new life in New York City, where most of the big agencies were located, but the first place to offer me a job was Ketchum, McLeod & Grove in Pittsburgh.

I was ready to try being an account executive like the men in the suits whom I had admired. At Harrill & Farr the owner had been the sole rainmaker and it hadn't taken me long to figure out the now clichéd business golden rule: He who has the gold—or brings in the gold—makes the rules. This is a strategy that has repeated itself throughout my career and is certainly one of the primary reasons for my rapid advancement—see who has the power, and work your tail off to be that person. Even if I didn't always know where I was headed, I did know that I never wanted to stay in one place. I wanted to keep learning, to keep getting better all the time, and measuring myself against those around me helped me to know that I was.

The people at Ketchum flew me up for an interview, which impressed me right off the bat. I was only about twenty-three at the time and I'd never had anyplace court me before. I went up there hoping to convince them to hire me as an assistant account executive so I could get some training in that area and eventually move up to being an account executive. In my interview, I showed them my portfolio and really wowed them by talking about the strategy behind each one of the ads that I'd done. They said they liked my passion and thought I had good instincts, so, despite my lack of experience, they offered me a job as a full-fledged account executive. I accepted right away, and Wendy and I packed up our things and headed for Pittsburgh.

Learn by Doing (or How I Created
My Own Business Degree)

At Ketchum I worked for Tom James, a Columbia MBA who had worked for Procter & Gamble and who knew as much about marketing as anyone I've ever met. He was also a great teacher. He'd even written a training manual on marketing, so essentially, he taught me his book. Probably the two most important things I learned from Tom were:

- *Critical Analysis, or How to Write Short Memos:* I fancied myself a writer, but under Tom I would rewrite test-market analyses six or seven times until I learned how to put forth a recommendation, explain the rationale for that recommendation, and summarize it all in a single page. I try to force myself to use this same discipline today. Limiting myself to a single page not only helps concentrate my mind, it almost guarantees clarity.

- *The Definition of Marketing:* When you get rid of all the doublespeak surrounding the finer points of marketing, what marketing really comes down to is convincing people to do something you want them to do. Today my marketing mantra is: "What consumer perception, habit, or belief do you have to either change, build, or reinforce in order to grow the business?" (When we answer that question, we always hit pay dirt. For instance, Taco Bell is breaking the hamburger habit by getting customers to, as our ad campaign puts it, "think outside the bun," which has really rung the register for the brand.)

My first account at Ketchum was Rockwell Power Tools, which was a bit ironic because I can barely change a drill bit. The first business presentation I gave was to the head of marketing for Rockwell International, and I was just awful. I was extremely nervous, and I must have said "you know" a thousand times during a fifteen-minute presentation. Fortunately, these were all roll-up-your-sleeves type guys, so they were very forgiving. They knew I was passionate and really cared about the business, and that can make up for a lot of sins early in your career. Still, flubbing that first presentation was a big deal for me that took years to get over. I realized then that there is no substitute for experience and for knowing your stuff, so I worked even harder to make sure I never messed up like that again. I also learned that it takes a while to get back up on the horse once your confidence is shattered and that there's nothing you can do about that except keep trying.

It was at Ketchum that I discovered that the big accounts were in packaged goods, so I decided that that's where I wanted to be. Packaged goods, such as Kraft cheese slices or Nabisco Oreos, are products that are sold to the consumer directly through supermarkets, and they are a high-velocity business, meaning products need to fly off the shelves. This virtually guaranteed bigger ad budgets and greater consumer awareness. After my first year Tom put me on the Heinz 57 account, which was a big break for me because it introduced me to a whole new level of sophistication. At Heinz, everyone had so much experience, and even though I was a junior person on the account, I learned a lot by just being in the same room with them.

I was at Ketchum for only a couple of years, but it's where I really got grounded in the fundamentals of the business. Still, I knew it wasn't the major leagues, and I was anxious to keep growing. I decided again to try to land a job with one of the big New York agencies. This time I could claim some big-time account experience, and with Tom's help, I got interviews and job offers from several major agencies.

Even though I thought I knew what I wanted, when I went up to New York to meet with people, I felt uncomfortable. Maybe it stemmed a bit from my own insecurity, but I sensed a real arrogance in the New York shops, like I was this hick-from-the-sticks and they were the ones with all the right answers. Besides that, it seemed like everyone there had an MBA, and because I was just a kid from the Midwest with only a bachelor's degree, no one was going to chance letting me work on any of the big accounts for quite a while.

Back then I used to excuse myself and go to the bathroom every time I was in a room with people who started talking about where they'd earned their business degrees. When that happened, I never felt like I fit in. (It also didn't help that I looked even younger than my age, which led me to make the really bad mistake of growing an embarrassing mustache.) Looking back, though, I realize that the arrogance that can come from having a pedigree can also keep you from noticing raw talent. I remember that now when I'm hiring people. A pedigree can't do the work for you, and some of the biggest hiring mistakes I've made have come from the fact that I assumed, because someone went to a name school and had impressive credentials, that that person could also get things done. In business, where you've been is a lot less important than what you can do. You get paid to deliver results.

Luckily for me, after I got back from New York I got a call from a headhunter who told me about an agency in Dallas called Tracy Locke that was looking for someone to handle its Frito-Lay account. The job would involve running the campaign for a new product that had just launched called Tostitos. It wasn't New York, but it was a highly visible, national account, and it was packaged goods. Besides, I loved the idea of going to Dallas. It was a city that was growing by leaps and bounds, and that's what I wanted to do.

I jumped at the chance, and it turned out to be a great move for me because it was my first exposure to PepsiCo, which owns Frito-Lay. I got promoted almost immediately to account executive for one of its biggest brands, Doritos. This was around the time that Doritos had a very successful campaign featuring the comedian Avery Schreiber, who would crunch on a Dorito, causing the buildings in the background to topple to the ground. One of my first responsibilities there was to come up with new and innovative ways for people to crunch and make things fall down—what we called "the crunch consequences." One of my favorite ideas was when we had a *Tyrannosaurus rex* skeleton crash through the floor when the museum curator crunched a chip. The look on his face was priceless.

This was also my first experience with branded line extensions. The original Doritos flavor was toasted corn, but then they came out with their Nacho Cheese flavor. It was such a big hit, the company wanted more. I was on the team charged with finding new flavor ideas, and we began our research in the salad-dressing aisle of our local supermarket. The bottled-salad-dressing business is all about creating taste sensations that are so potent, the fact that they might overwhelm everything they're put on is actually considered a plus. Ranch dressing was the top-selling salad-dressing flavor at the time, so we thought, "Why not try it on a chip?"

Once we decided on the right flavor, we needed a name that would appeal to customers. We call it bringing a unique image to a known quantity. We didn't just call the first line extension Cheese Doritos, we called it *Nacho* Cheese Doritos to give that extra punch. By the same token, we wanted something better than just Ranch Doritos for the new product, so we tried out all sorts of names. Out of that process, Cool Ranch Doritos were born.

Create a Sense of Urgency

At Tracy Locke I got to work directly for Howard Davis, who was the management supervisor for the Frito-Lay account. The first time I went down there to meet with him, he picked me up at the airport in his silver Corvette and whisked me off to this really nice restaurant, where he ordered wine for both of us as soon as we sat down. Howard was always like that—he liked to take charge of things, to make an impression. He was six feet four, with silver hair—the quintessential advertising guy. He had a glass-topped desk in his office because, as he put it, he liked to be able to look down and see his Guccis while he worked.

Howard taught me how to get things done. He was very smart but he was also an animal. He exuded power and could be very intimidating, and he knew how to use his power to get results while still managing to be a good guy. Howard's personal style was very different from my own, but what he did teach me was how to create a sense of urgency, how to motivate performance by getting everyone's heart pounding.

Howard could be tough and compassionate at the same time. My greatest memory of this involved an incident from my personal life. After nine years of marriage, Wendy got pregnant. She has had juvenile diabetes since she was seven, and back before insulin pumps, she used to give herself shots two or three times a day. When I proposed to her, I remember her saying, "You know, we'll never have kids. In fact, I may not even live past forty." I knew she had a terrible disease, but I didn't care because I was so much in love.

When she did get pregnant, it was a really scary time for us. Her body had a hard time handling both the diabetes and the pregnancy, and she got so sick that she was ordered to stay in bed. Ten weeks before the due date, I was at work in the middle of a presentation when I got the call that Wendy was at the hospital getting ready to deliver.

When our baby, Ashley, was born, she was only four pounds, ten ounces. The doctors warned me about all the possible complications, but when I first got to see her at the hospital, all I could think was how beautiful she was. I reached down to touch her with my finger, which she immediately grabbed and squeezed. Right then, I knew she was going to live.

When Ashley got older it became our ritual that when I

tucked her into bed, she would squeeze my finger to say good night. She really got me on her wedding day when she grabbed my finger just as I gave her away. In my office, I still have a picture of the two of us right after she was born. My hand looks huge behind her tiny head, and she has tape over her mouth and tubes coming out of her. That picture reminds me every day of what's really important in life.

Wendy lost her eyesight for a while afterward and had to have several operations to fix it. I stayed with her and Ashley every day, and since the doctors told us that studies showed that the more you're there, the more likely the child will live, I talked to Ashley all the time. Wendy and I even made tapes of us talking so the nurses could play them to Ashley when we needed to sleep. It was days before we knew she was going to be okay, but she finally made it, and we took her home in doll clothes because she was still so small.

Howard, as demanding as he was, gathered everyone in the company as soon as Wendy went into the hospital, explained what I was going through, and then told them that he would fire anyone who called me while all this was going on. That definitely created a sense of urgency because everybody rallied around the cause and figured out how to compensate for my absence. No matter how much easier it would have been for them to call me up and ask me this question about one of my accounts or where that important document was, they all just took care of things.

Howard proved that being a tough motivator who gets things done and being a decent person aren't mutually exclusive. The support I got at work was overwhelming, and I've never forgotten it. If anyone on my team today has a family emergency, we just move heaven and earth to help. We've even gone so far as to lend a number of people the corporate plane when they need to get to a funeral or take a family member to another city for medical treatment. I learned early on that health and family have got to come first. It's the right thing to do, and besides, no one can be good on the job when he's preoccupied with what's happening at home.

Help Make It "Their" Idea

You may think you're not influenced by advertising, but if you've ever bought a brand-name drug rather than the much cheaper generic, if you own an iPod rather than one of the less expensive players, then the fact is you probably are. In fact, there's a $100 billion industry that's betting on it.

At Tracy Locke, I met a creative director named Ian Fawn-Meade who had this take on advertising called "the third idea." In advertising there's always the emotional side, which appeals to your heart, and the rational side, which appeals to your brain. These are the first two ideas. The third idea is the one that buyers come up with on their own. You can tell people to go out and buy something, but that doesn't make them do it. But if you appeal to both the head and the heart in a compelling and relevant way, then people will come up with the idea to buy of their own accord.

Think of the way a company like Nike never tells you to go out and buy its shoes because they are among the highest-performing athletic shoes on the market. In fact, they often use very little language in their commercials. Instead, they put their shoes on high-performing athletes, and you immediately get the picture. Then you think to yourself, "If I want to play basketball to the best of my abilities, maybe I should get those sneakers, too."

I say to people all the time that telling isn't selling. What we often strive for in our restaurant commercials is what we call "lick-the-screen images," beautiful food photography that makes people salivate over our food without us having to tell them the obvious—that our products taste great.

This idea of self-discovery, or coming up with something on your own, would become a very big concept for me, and once I had learned enough about it I would pass it on to others, because I think that is the key to acquiring knowledge. I don't think that as a leader you just go tell people to do something. I believe you plant the seeds and share with them what you know and let them draw their own conclusions—which may even be better than your own.

Act Like a Leader

When I got promoted to be in charge of the entire Frito-Lay business, the agency's largest and most important account, I was only twenty-seven years old, a good ten years younger than the clients I was dealing with.

I was a little rough around the edges, so the agency decided I could use some more polish. They sent me to an "image consultant" in Dallas by the name of Jack Byrum.

Jack Byrum was a legend. He had worked with Johnny Carson as well as high-powered business types, including most of the higher-ups at Pepsi. His thing was what he called "the main man" idea: When you walk into a room, you want to exude authority, you want everyone to know that you are the main man. Byrum was the one who invented that whole red-tie/blue-suit power look that all the corporate players had adopted for a time.

Jack Byrum taught me a lot of useful things about personal style and self-awareness, about being more conscious of who my audience is and the image that I want to project as a result. This doesn't mean trying to be someone other than who you are, but it does mean becoming more aware of your personality traits, both good and bad, and how, in any particular situation, you might want to modify them to come across in a particular way.

For instance, I have a tendency to become overly enthused, to get so excited about something I start talking faster and flapping my arms around. While this may be fine if I'm making a sales presentation, it's probably going to be less well received if I'm talking to a group of financial analysts. Jack explained to me that I needed, not to get rid of that part of myself, but to use it in such a way as to make it more effective, more relevant to a particular business situation. So I should keep my enthusiasm but learn how to temper it and display it appropriately. Today, I often tell our people to think of themselves as a brand and to be aware of the kind of image they want to project.

What Byrum had me do was watch videos of effective communicators such as "the Great Communicator" Ronald Reagan, who spoke so slowly and softly, he projected a quiet, reassuring confidence. (Can you imagine Ronald Reagan raising his voice?) And to help me focus on what I needed to work on in the future, he made me write down on three-by-five-inch index cards the answers to two questions: "What are you today?" and "What do you want to be tomorrow?" I still do this at the beginning of every year.

Keep a Lid on Your Ego

The biggest thing I learned from Jack Byrum was "Don't look up. Don't look down. Always look straight ahead."

What he meant by this harkens back to my earlier comments about "staying right-sized." No matter how high you get, you're no better than anyone else (which is another way of saying, "Stay grounded"), and no matter how low you are, you're no worse than anyone else. This may sound like common sense, but who hasn't at one time or another seen people try to intimidate others with their power? Conversely, who respects somebody who rolls over like Fluffy the dog? Byrum believed in projecting a powerful, "main man" image, but if your ego comes across as bigger than it ought to be, no one will see you as a credible leader.

Today, when I meet with younger people in our organization, I love it when they look me straight in the eye and tell me what they want to say, rather than what they think I want to hear. I think that's the greatest thing in the world, and it shows me that they're looking straight ahead.

Don't Intimidate or Let Yourself Be Intimidated

Part of always looking straight ahead is not being easily intimidated or trying to intimidate others. Toward the end of my advertising career—and this is probably part of the reason I decided to end it—I had to deal with a top executive at Frito-Lay who was one of the most brilliant people I have ever known but also one of the most arrogant, and intentionally intimidating.

If you said something he disagreed with, he'd simply look away as though you didn't exist. I remember presenting advertising copy to him that he obviously didn't like. But rather than tell me he didn't like it, he just started talking to someone else like I wasn't even in the room. He would almost always be at least ten minutes late for meetings, and it seemed clear to me that he did that just to show that he could and that nothing could happen without him. (It's probably one of the reasons I try to be obsessively punctual today.)

Wendy knew how I felt about this guy, but she also knew I could never say anything to him because he was the client. One time she and I ended up sitting next to him at a wedding reception. Wendy was working for a local TV station at the time, and he was giving her all sorts of grief about what was wrong with their local newscast—the sports came on too late, the weather came on too early, blah blah. Wendy didn't know much about him other than that he was "the father of Grandma's Cookies," which were soft-baked cookies that were meant to taste homemade. He had launched Grandma's Cookies into an overcrowded marketplace with no success. In fact, they had been a colossal failure.

Finally, after about twenty minutes of being harassed, Wendy turned to him and said, "Who told you the world needed another soft cookie?"

I just about died. This guy was important to my career, and at that point, as far as he was concerned, we ceased to exist for the rest of the reception. But secretly, I was envious. Wendy had done what I had always been too afraid to do—put him in his place.

Not too long after this, I decided that I had pretty much had it with advertising. I had learned a lot, I had met a lot of great people, but at some point it just takes too much out of you. I got tired of making recommendations all the time and wanted to have some control over what actually got done.

One incident kind of crystallized this frustration for me. It was a campaign we were doing for Doritos, and I thought the work was just terrible. I expressed my opinion to my agency colleagues, but I was told in no uncertain terms that my job was to sell it.

So I went over to Frito-Lay and presented the work to Leo Kiely, who is now CEO of Coors. "How could you bring this to me?" Leo asked.

I said, "Well, this is the agency's point of view."

Leo said, "I know you, David. I know you don't like this work."

I just kept saying, "Well, it's the agency's point of view" because there was nothing else I could say to defend it.

Right about then, I flashed back to high school when I sold those encyclopedias no one needed door-to-door and how bad I had felt about that. Now Leo was saying to me, "David, I want the truth. Are you telling me that you like this work, that you really believe in the campaign, and that you are recommending we go with it?"

I said, "Leo, you're right. I don't really like the work, but my job is not to like it; it's to sell it."

Once I said it out loud, I knew I couldn't go on. I needed to find a place where I had some ownership over the ideas I was promoting to ensure that they were things that I truly believed in.

Stay True to Your Convictions

That's the moment I knew it was time to move on. I knew I couldn't effectively sell work I didn't believe in. Mark Wyse, who was married to the bestselling author and legendary copywriter Lois Wyse, once told a story about standing up for your convictions even if it's about nothing more than advertising copy.

The Wyses were pitching the Smucker's jelly account, which is based in Cleveland, and Lois had come up with this brilliant copy line: "With a name like Smucker's, it has to be good." At the time it was still a family-owned business, so the question was: How smart is it to pitch a product by making fun of the owner's name? The safe route would have been to come up with something else, but it was such a great line, the Wyses decided to go with it anyway.

The Smucker's marketing people were highly offended and came right out and said so, but Mr. Smucker got it right away. However, because the family name was so well respected throughout the state, he said, "You can use it everywhere except in Ohio."

The campaign was a big hit, and that tagline became instantly recognizable throughout the country. Soon after that, Mr. Smucker was on a plane flying to California. A very attractive flight attendant happened to notice his boarding pass and said to him, "Oh, Mr. Smucker. With a name like that, you've got to be good!"

The first thing Mr. Smucker did when he got off the plane was call Mark Wyse and tell him, "Let's start using that slogan in Ohio."

Today, I know the one essential character trait of any leader is personal integrity. And if I had to feel some discomfort the way I did in Leo Kiely's office that day in order to figure this out, well, better sooner than later.

I had gotten to the point where I wanted to be the man making the decisions, the one who would say, "This is great work" or "I know you can do better."

Maybe it was time for me to become the main man.

5

The A-Team

Learning from the Best

T
he most remarkable thing about my transition from the agency business to corporate America, as embodied by PepsiCo, one of the world's great companies, is how unremarkable it was.

I have never been short on ambition, and in one way or another, I had been working toward a big career jump from the very beginning. There's a difference between ambition and blind ambition, and even though I've been blessed enough to have many opportunities come my way over the years, I was also always looking two or three moves ahead to get an idea of where I might want to go next. That's why getting put on the PepsiCo-owned Frito-Lay account had been such a big deal for me. I knew it could lead to bigger things.

This was at a time when PepsiCo made every list of the world's best companies—one of the "most admired companies," one of the "best companies to work for," one of the "smartest companies," and so on. To my mind, PepsiCo was the A-team, and I was thrilled to be a part of it.

What happened is that a position opened up in Pepsi-Co's restaurant division for senior vice president of marketing at Pizza Hut. Leo Kiely—the same Leo who had asked me, "Do you like this work, David?"—and Frito-Lay's president, Bill Korn, recommended me to Steve Reinemund, who was president of Pizza Hut.

It's Not What You Know or Who You Know—It's Both

When I flew to Wichita, Kansas, to meet Steve Reinemund for the first time, he picked me up at the airport and actually carried my bag. I figured either he was a really nice, humble guy or he really needed a marketing person. It turned out both were true.

Steve and I hit it off immediately, and he offered me the job based on the work I'd done for Frito-Lay. But first I had to go meet with the top brass at PepsiCo to get the final nod. I had gotten to know Wayne Calloway, chairman of PepsiCo, because Wendy and I played tennis with him and his wife, Jan. And I knew Mike Jordan, who was also way up there (and is now the CEO of EDS), so when I arrived for my interview, it was not so much "Why should we hire you?" as it was "When do you want to start?"

Did the fact that I knew all these people help me get the job? Absolutely. But they all also knew and respected my work. That's the thing about connections. I had courted these relationships, there's no doubt about it. And I had worked at turning them into friendships. But if the people who can help your career don't like and respect your work, then these relationships can only work against you.

When I was working with the folks at Frito-Lay, I always made a point of being more prepared than was probably necessary. I took every opportunity to define my role as broadly as possible, putting myself in the mind frame of their head of marketing rather than just somebody from the ad agency they had hired. I played a lead role in helping to develop their annual operating plans, for example, even though that wasn't strictly part of my job. When I presented a new idea, I always had contingency plans and backup ideas. Even if they were never used, the fact that I had given them some thought made an impression. Today I tell my people all the time that just doing the job well is the baseline. It's what you do above and beyond what's expected of you that gets you noticed. Leo Kiely always paid me this great compliment. He'd say, "You're one of the best marketing people at Frito-Lay, and you don't even work here."

Ambition Is Great but Don't Flaunt It

So I became the head of marketing for one of the world's largest restaurant chains at the ripe old age of thirty-four. Later, I would become CEO of a twenty-billion-dollar company at the age of forty-six. I am often asked how I was able to advance through the ranks so quickly.

I really am one of those great believers in the power of positive thinking. You become what you think you can become. First you dream what you can become. Then, as you get more and more experience, you become it.

As I said before, everything's relative. You have to constantly be looking at the people around you and measuring your performance against theirs. If someone's better than you, then you have to do what you can to learn how to be as good as that person, and then how to be better. If someone's as smart and experienced as you, then you work harder because when all things are equal, the person who works the hardest always has the edge. One thing I've learned over the years is that you never get promoted until most people in your company can already see you in the position. I knew I was going to become president of a PepsiCo division when someone else got promoted to president of Pizza Hut and my phone started ringing off the hook with people asking me if I was upset that it hadn't been me.

I hadn't thought too much about being president up until that point, but I have to admit, once I got the idea in my head, I got a little carried away with it. Suddenly, and rather randomly, I decided it was really important that, by the age of forty, I become president of something.

I wasn't too circumspect about this ambition. In fact, I kind of wore it on my sleeve—letting the world know that hard-charging David Novak was a guy to be reckoned with.

One day, the aforementioned chairman of PepsiCo, Wayne Calloway, took me aside and said to me, "David, I have no doubt that one day you *are* going to end up running something. So why don't you just focus on what you need to do today in order to be ready when you get there."

Sometimes a guy needs to get hit by a two-by-four to get him back on track. I decided to keep my nose to the grindstone after that and to let my results speak for themselves.

Opportunity Attracts Talent

It is always more difficult to make an immediate impact on a company that is near or at the top of its game than on one that is not, and for whatever reasons, it seems that every new place I've gone to was experiencing some sort of trouble.

The good news for me was that when I joined Pizza Hut, it was going through a very rough patch. Sales were down. The relationship with the franchisees wasn't great. The delivery business was losing money. And Domino's was kicking our butt.

The bad news, on the face of it, was that Pizza Hut was headquartered in Wichita, Kansas. This is not to denigrate the good people of Wichita, but when you're trying to attract top talent, Wichita is not considered one of the world's business Meccas.

Yet again, I discovered how very wrong I can be. I ended up putting together one of the best marketing departments ever assembled, not just among PepsiCo companies but in the whole of corporate America. Virtually everyone who worked in that department went on to become a superstar.

We recruited people from General Mills and Procter & Gamble and from cosmopolitan areas like Chicago and Minneapolis. Bill McDonald, who is now head of marketing for Capital One, came there. So did Steve Farley, the future head of marketing for JCPenney. We had Jeff Moody, who went on to become CEO of the Subway Franchise Association; Terry Davenport, who'd later become the head of strategy for Starbucks; and Ken Caldwell, the future head of marketing at Domino's. They all came to the middle of nowhere to be part of something special.

What I discovered, of course, is that if people think they will have good opportunities and a chance to grow, they will come. Having lived and worked all over the place, I now believe that geography is way overrated as it relates to happiness. If you are happy with and challenged by your work, you will be happy doing it on the moon.

We had a blast at Pizza Hut. It is so much fun and so gratifying to turn a company around, and that's what we were doing. When I first got there, there was nothing new in terms of marketing and products, nothing for the customers to get excited about, so we developed an advertising campaign called "Makin' it great," which became our rallying cry. Then we improved our prices to be competitive in the delivery category. We introduced specialty pizzas—Meat Lover's, Cheese Lover's, Pepperoni Lover's. That was a huge success. All this really drove traffic.

Back then everyone was saying you couldn't do kids' marketing because McDonald's owned it. Nobody else was even trying it because no one thought they could compete, but I said, "That's crazy, let's take a stab at it." So we created kids' nights: If you brought your kids in, each of them got a free personal pan pizza along with balloons and a little party kit. All of a sudden, we were getting weekend volumes on Tuesday nights.

Then we did promotions. We did a tie-in with *The Land Before Time,* the animated dinosaur movie. We sold these little dinosaur puppets for ninety-nine cents with the purchase of a pizza. We broke sales records in December when we had those dinosaurs because Pizza Hut had never done that before.

Next we did tie-ins with the NCAA basketball tournament. We created these mini-basketballs with the NCAA logo for that year that we sold for about $2.99 with the purchase of a pizza. We sold close to six million of them in a four-week period. Again, the result was record sales, and it was a promotion we did successfully for years.

What I also discovered was that, in any customer-centric business, if you can make the customer happy, then everyone else is going to be happy as well. Customers drive sales, and sales are a tangible measure that you are succeeding. Happy customers make for happy employees, happy managers, happy CEOs, and ultimately, happy investors. Of course, most people already know this, and the kinds of promotions and marketing initiatives that we started at Pizza Hut weren't exactly radical new ideas in the restaurant industry. But there is a big difference between knowing and doing, and at Pizza Hut, no one had been doing much of anything before I got there. My team started paying attention to what worked for the competition and figured out how to make it work for us. They were great at coming up with new ways to drive the business, and we proved that not only could these kinds of things work at Pizza Hut, but they could work big.

Enthusiasm Is Contagious

Because I take a great many days each year to personally present a leadership seminar to as many of our people as I can possibly accommodate, I've spent a lot of time thinking about my own abilities to lead. As much as I would love for people to cite my IQ or my strategic thinking or even my propensity for hard work as my finest asset, I have to admit that I've been told my number-one quality as a leader is my infectious enthusiasm. What does enthusiasm have to do with leadership? Just about everything. Positive energy always arouses loyalty and enthusiasm in others.

When I first got to Pizza Hut, it was probably my unbridled enthusiasm, however unintentional, that started to turn things around. I had been on board no more than a couple of months when I had to go out to San Diego to address our franchisees.

In any franchise business, there always seems to be some natural tension between the franchisees, the entrepreneurs who own and run individual restaurants, and the people at the parent company, the corporate types who develop the marketing programs and operations processes for the brand. Apparently, the presentation the year before had been something of a disaster. Word had come back that some of the franchisees didn't think the Pizza Hut team came off as real, that its presentations were too canned. There was a lot of pressure on us to perform.

To stir things up, we decided to change the entire presentation into an interview format. We hired a lookalike of David Hartman (who for many years had been the co-host of ABC's *Good Morning America*) to be our interviewer of a show called *Pizza Hut Today*. The idea was that each of us would provide him with our questions, and he would proceed to "interview" us for the presentation.

When my turn came, I didn't take a single note up onstage with me. I was wearing one of those little microphones, and when I started talking about all the new marketing things we were going to do, I got so excited, I kind of got my hands going. The next thing I knew, I had knocked my mike about halfway across the stage.

Well, the franchisees ate it up. Everyone laughed and kidded me about it afterward. Not only had they responded to my enthusiasm, I had come off as a real person rather than a corporate robot. At that point, I had already been out in the field and met a lot of the franchisees and listened to what they had to say. But this is what got me into the club, quite literally. At these conventions the franchisees always had a private suite for playing cards; they called it the Milk & Cookies Room. They tell me I was the first corporate type who ever came to their room, although I wasn't actually invited. I just walked in and made myself at home.

One final word about my enthusiasm. I can get so carried away that, as the boss, I have to be ever vigilant to remain open to other people's points of view. Just because I'm enthusiastic doesn't necessarily mean I'm right. I have to always keep the doors open for honest communication, or I could enthusiastically lead everyone right over the cliff.

Reward and Recognize, Part 1

I learned at Pizza Hut that my enthusiasm would take things only so far. Getting people geared up to turn business around was just the first step. After that, I had to find a way to sustain that energy in my team and keep the momentum going.

I discovered that getting everyone involved was key. I started monthly department meetings where everyone would come together to talk about the business, share what we knew, and brainstorm about how to solve problems. It's not like this was a revolutionary idea, but oddly enough, no other department at Pizza Hut was doing anything like it at the time. Most of our new marketing and promotion ideas, like the tie-in to the NCAA basketball championships, came out of those meetings.

It was for those monthly meetings that I created my very first recognition award, a motivation tool that I've used everywhere I've worked since and that has become a defining part of our culture at Yum! Brands. My first award was called the Traveling Pan, and it was a simple thing. I got this big silver pizza pan that I awarded to someone each month by inscribing their name on it for a job well done. The next month, a new person got it, and I added his or her name to the list. The "awarding of the pan" became a mini-ceremony each month at the end of our meetings, and everyone loved it. Even if most of the meeting was about solving some particularly difficult problem, everyone knew that there was at least part of that meeting that they could look forward to.

It was such a successful tool for making people feel appreciated and motivated to do a good job that people in other departments heard about it and the idea spread. Steve Reinemund, the president of Pizza Hut, wanted to find a way to celebrate the managers of those restaurants that were bringing in the most money each year, so he came up with the idea for the Million-Dollar Manager coats. Somewhat in the tradition of the Masters golf tournament, the managers of those restaurants that made a million dollars in sales that year were flown in for a special ceremony where they were given a coat and inducted into the Million-Dollar Managers Club. Seeing the pride on people's faces when they received their award was really inspiring.

From then on, I was hooked and would make reward and recognition one of my primary focuses as a leader. It doesn't matter whether you're dealing with a highly ranked executive or someone who's taking orders in a restaurant; you can never underestimate the power of telling someone he's doing a good job. And according to some human relations experts, in many cases, it's even more important than money.

You'd Better Have a Sense of Humor

Do you need to be a control freak in order to be an effective CEO? I certainly know plenty of good CEOs who are.

And while certain controlling tendencies have helped me get to where I am today, I believe one of the greatest challenges to any leader is learning how to let go, to understand and appreciate that you can't get there alone. It is why I commit so much time to teaching my leadership program to as many people in our organization as I possibly can. It's designed to help people realize their goals and bring out their best qualities as leaders, which is why I call it Taking People with You. A CEO, or any leader for that matter, has to accept that the only way to achieve desired goals is through other people.

Okay, I'm also very competitive, which is where those controlling tendencies come from. I hate to lose. I hate to be wrong. I hate having to accept it when I am wrong. But I learned fairly early on that being wrong is part of life and is probably life's greatest teacher.

I also learned that you'd better not take yourself too seriously. Things go wrong every day, "the best-laid plans of mice and men" and so on, and if you don't have a sense of humor about yourself, then one day you are just going to implode.

My stint as marketing director of Pizza Hut was the scene of my first big public business disaster. In 1989 we were on an incredible roll, and I was feeling pretty full of myself. We were coming off those very successful tie-in promotions when we were given the opportunity to tie in with what was shaping up to be the major movie blockbuster of the Christmas season, *Back to the Future Part II*.

It seemed like it would be be a slam-dunk. *Back to the Future* had blown the top out at the box office—it had even been made into an amusement-park ride at Universal's theme parks—and had made Michael J. Fox a movie star.

For our promotion, we decided to create these really hip sunglasses, a wraparound, futuristic, reflective model that we were going to call solar shades. When you do a movie tie-in, you commit millions in advertising and promotion dollars, so you wrap it up pretty tight with the movie's producers about the way in which the product is going to be featured. We envisioned Michael J. Fox wearing these cool shades in the movie and every kid in America wanting a pair.

So we ordered *nine million* pairs of solar shades.

My first inkling that this might be something less than the total blowout that I'd envisioned was when I brought home a pair of these sunglasses for my daughter, Ashley, who was around eight years old at the time. Ashley's reaction was: "Dad, these are really dorky. Who'd ever wear them? Besides, everybody already has sunglasses."

That took me aback. I'd figured that sunglasses were a fashion statement at any age, which is why you're more likely to see nine million *styles* of sunglasses rather than nine million pairs of one style. But what the heck. This was just one kid's opinion even if she just happened to be my daughter.

We had arranged to have the *Back to the Future Part II* premiere in Wichita, which, as you can imagine, was a pretty big deal. We made it a black-tie event and even brought in the silver DeLorean gull-winged car, which had been one of the "stars" of both movies. I still have a picture of my family, all wearing solar shades, standing next to that car.

We had two showings because we'd invited all our

employees and their families to come. Before the first one, I got up, wearing those glasses, to welcome everyone and then sat back down to enjoy the movie.

As I watched, I waited for our glasses to show up. I waited. I waited. And then I waited some more. Once, I saw some kid in the background riding a bike who may have had on a pair, although I couldn't be sure. Otherwise, the glasses never showed up.

Almost as bad was that I was sitting next to Steve Reinemund, Pizza Hut's president. *Back to the Future Part II* had a risqué hot-tub scene and some X-rated language. Steve got upset, not just because the glasses never showed up, but also because we'd invited all these families with little kids. The first thing he said to me after the movie was, "We've got to get a letter out to everyone apologizing for this right away." So I went home that night and, rather than celebrate what was supposed to be a great moment of triumph, composed a letter of apology to the entire company.

The next day, I called up one of the movie's producers and asked her what happened to our sunglasses, but it didn't really matter. It was too late. I suppose we could have sued, but what good would it have done? We'd been taken to the cleaners.

Shortly after that, I was in Chicago talking to one of our restaurant managers and I asked him if there was anything we could do for him back at headquarters. "Yeah," he said, "there sure is. You can fire whoever the guy is who came up with that stupid sunglasses promotion."

Eventually, we got rid of most of the solar shades, though it took us about a year. I realized after that experience that I had gotten a little too cocky for my own good. I should have known that just because my team was on a roll didn't mean that things couldn't still go terribly wrong, and I should have made more of an effort to test out the idea, ask for opinions, before going so far out on a limb. I also realized that when you make a mistake that big, it can stay with you for a long time, so you'd better be able to laugh it off. I still catch flack about those sunglasses today. Recently, one of our franchisees attended my leadership seminar and said to me, "I got a little something for you." Sure enough, he pulled out a pair of those darn solar shades!

6

My Own Private Cola Wars

Paying My Dues

Today's PepsiCo is the result of a merger in 1965 between Frito-Lay and Pepsi-Cola. The company then acquired Pizza Hut, Taco Bell, and Kentucky Fried Chicken, resulting in three divisions: beverages, snack foods, and restaurants.

The divisions were supposedly equal, but beverage was really "more equal" than the others. It was the crown prince of PepsiCo's empire. Because of my team's success at Pizza Hut—we doubled sales and profits while I was there and completely turned around the delivery business—Roger Enrico asked me to transfer to the beverage division and offered me the job of executive vice president of marketing and sales, which meant leaving Wichita for New York. I jumped at the chance, probably a little too quickly. Steve Reinemund, the president of Pizza Hut, wasn't at all happy about my leaving because there wasn't an obvious replacement.

I should have involved him more in the process rather than just handing it to him as a done deal. He had given me my first opportunity at PepsiCo, and I owed him a lot more sensitivity. He had championed me from day one and had taken the time to teach me everything he knew about the restaurant business, which was a lot. Still, I couldn't wait to get on the next ship. It took us a while to reestablish a good relationship after that, and that was my bad. Years later my KFC marketing head jumped ship on me to go to Taco Bell, and I didn't like it one bit either. It was only then that I fully realized why Steve was so miffed.

Who the Heck Is Wojak?

While I was excited by the opportunity, I accepted the job with some trepidation. The head of marketing for Pepsi-Cola was a highly visible position, but it came with a certain amount of risk—a real up-and-out possibility. Roger Enrico had been the last one to make it work, and the four people who followed him had all been canned or moved to another job. In fact, there was one brief moment when I thought my tenure was going to be shorter than anyone's.

On my first day, I picked up the newspaper and read the following headline: "Wojak Named Head of Pepsi Marketing." Damn, I finally got my name in lights, and it was misspelled to the point of being unrecognizable! At least I wasn't as upset as my mom and dad.

I should have taken that as a sign of things to come. In the beginning, everything about my new position felt a bit off the mark. Here I was with this big job and a big office at one of the world's most impressive companies, but almost immediately I thought I might have made a big mistake. Pepsi was much more hierarchical than Pizza Hut, and the working environment was much more aloof. There were 225 people in the marketing department, and to this day I'm not sure what most of them did. Whenever I wanted to do something, there was always someone there saying, "Oh don't worry. We'll take care of that for you." At Pepsi it seemed to be that the higher up you got, the less you were supposed to do. I was much more hands-on than that, much more of a doer. I didn't want to make all the decisions, but I definitely wanted to be more involved than my predecessors.

I was also having trouble communicating what I wanted to get done. When I first got there, for instance, I was telling people about the Traveling Pan Award at Pizza Hut and how I wanted to do something similar at Pepsi. Then one of my helpful marketing staffers said, "Why don't you let us figure out a good recognition award for you?" They came back with this very expensive-looking laminated plaque with the Pepsi-Cola logo on it, the kind of thing you'd throw into the back of your closet the first chance you got. It was self-important, completely lacking in the kind of fun and creativity I was looking for, but I went along with it be-cause I figured it was the Pepsi way.

Those first few months at Pepsi really threw me off my game. In fact, I would have to say that that brief period was the only time in my career where I didn't look for-ward to coming to work every morning.

Sometimes you have to go through the pain of not en-joying your job and just persevere. At Pizza Hut, I had a lot of fun and made things happen, but at Pepsi the culture was so entrenched, it took me a while to figure out how to break through and actually get something done myself.

Find a Way

Imagine you're trying to get inside a house. The front door is locked, so you try the back door, and that's locked too. You try all the windows and they're all shut tight. This is starting to get a little annoying, but here's the thing: You already *see* yourself inside that house. You might have to pull out a vent, you might have to find a broken basement window, you might even have to go down the chimney. But one way or another, you are going to get inside that house. How you ultimately do it is just so much detail.

Finding a way to get something done might be the number one skill of a leader. It's not so much "Don't take no for an answer" as it is finding acceptable alternatives, looking for all the other ways to skin a cat. The leader may have to go under, over, around, or right through the middle, but one way or another he's going to find a way—he's going to get inside that house.

This was sort of the situation I found myself in at Pepsi. I had to find a way to start getting things done. The answer was Mountain Dew.

Mountain Dew was the one brand Pepsi owned that I thought had a lot more going for it than we realized. It has a unique flavor, and I thought more people would love it if we could get them to try it. Consumers loved its jolt.

But the way it had been marketed from the beginning actually seemed to have limited its potential. It was perceived as unsophisticated, very country, and the well-established advertising guidelines perpetuated this notion by insisting that all Mountain Dew advertising include some sort of water imagery—mountain lakes, running streams, and the like.

I thought Mountain Dew needed a new image, but even though I was leading marketing, I couldn't get Alan Pottasch, the legendary head of Pepsi advertising and the father of "the Pepsi Generation," to change his mind on this point. Alan's approach had been very successful in the past, so it was totally understandable why he was reluctant to go a different way, but my gut told me we could do a whole lot better. So I went around the system and had another legend, Phil Dusenberry, the head of the BBDO agency, create an advertising campaign for Diet Mountain Dew instead, which was this little brand that no one was paying much attention to. Phil and his team created an urban campaign that featured "the Dew Boys" whose tagline was "Been there, done that." People picked up on that phrase right away and started using it all over the place. Creating an expression that becomes part of the vernacular is every marketer's dream. I still smile today every time I hear someone say, "Been there, done that."

That campaign ignited sales, and Diet Mountain Dew became our fastest-growing beverage. That evolved into the Mountain Dew "Do the Dew" campaign, which was edgier and more energetic, centered on extreme sports like mountain climbing and skateboarding, and it was also very successful. I was beginning to make things happen in the Pepsi system, and I was back on my game.

Understand the *Real* Issue

Another thing that I think often happens in big companies is that you get so used to looking at a problem in a certain way that everybody buys into the same point of view, so that the simplest or the best or the most obvious or creative solution is the last one to occur to you. Sometimes what the problem needs is a fresh pair of eyes.

Wayne Calloway was the chairman of PepsiCo while I was there, and he would always ask at meetings, "When are we going to get into the water business?" Every time he saw me, he'd also pull me aside and say, "David, when are we going to get into the water business?" After the chairman asks the same question several times, you would think that coming up with an answer might be a pretty good idea. But we kept shooting blanks.

In the early nineties, bottled water was the fastest-growing segment of the beverage business. We knew it was unlikely we were going to discover some exotic, untapped mountain spring somewhere, so we got hung up on the idea of acquiring a company that had already figured out this business. It took us forever to see the obvious: that it wasn't where the water came from that the consumer cared about, it was the purity. My immediate boss, Craig Weatherup, took the lead on this. In fairly short order, we figured out a way to purify the water we were already using at our Pepsi bottling plants without the expense of aquiring a mountain spring water, and we created Aquafina, which is now the number one brand of water in the world.

Give Others the Credit

What was interesting about this is that Wayne Calloway never asked for or received one ounce of credit for our success, although he was the one who came up with the idea and kept pushing us toward it. He let us have all the glory. I learned from Wayne that success is a tangible asset that leaders use to make others feel good about themselves.

I think that when you're young, you want to establish yourself as someone who can get things done, so getting credit for your work is important. But the higher up the ladder you are, the more important it is to give credit rather than receive it. I believe that it's much more important, and better for business, to celebrate the successes of others than to crow about your own. That's why I love telling people about the great things happening in our company that I had nothing to do with. One of my favorites is how Gregg Dedrick, the president of KFC, came up with the idea for the fast-food product of the year in 2006. Gregg loves to mix all the food on his plate into one big pile and eat it all together, so he figured that if he likes to do that, then other people probably do, too. That's how our new Famous Bowls came about at KFC, layering items like mashed potatoes, popcorn chicken, corn, cheese, and gravy one atop the other in one bowl. I tell that story not just to make Gregg feel good but also to show people that I value new ideas and innovation so that they'll start thinking that way themselves.

Go from Me to We

Pepsi-Cola had always been a glitzy company, maybe the glitziest in the world. We always signed up the biggest celebrity of the moment, from M. C. Hammer to Madonna to Cindy Crawford to Michael Jackson (remember Michael

Jackson's hair catching fire during the filming of a pyrotechnic-heavy Pepsi commercial? That happened before I got there, thank God).

Pepsi got a lot of mileage out of its celebrity attachments. It was good for the brand's image, and it was good for company morale, too. But no one was really looking at what impact these expensive endorsements were having on recent sales, and the answer was fairly easy to find: Since Michael Jackson, not much. The things that had historically driven sales were product news, like introducing Diet Pepsi, and packaging news, like going from six-packs to twelve-packs to twenty-four-packs or from twelve-ounce bottles to sixteen-ounce bottles.

Of course, no one wanted to give up the glitz, which was integral to Pepsi's brand image. Instead, I said, "Okay, we'll still do the image-building celebrity stuff, but we need to keep pushing the more substantive marketing initiatives—the new products and the new ways to package." This resulted in swirl plastic bottles and a refrigerator pack we called "the cube."

One of our big celebrity endorsers was Magic Johnson, who had been our lead guy on Orange Slice and had also made an appearance in some Pepsi commercials. In 1991, soon after I joined Pepsi, Magic announced that he had been diagnosed as being HIV-positive. This was front-page news. People were dying left and right from AIDS, and there was a lot of fear because we didn't know much about the disease back then. A few NBA players were even refusing to play against Magic because he might get some of his blood on them. (He did voluntarily retire for a while, then returned to the game, then retired again.) Some of his endorsement deals were starting to fall through as well. We were getting a lot of calls from the press asking if we were going to keep him on or cut him loose.

Magic wanted to fly in from California to see where he stood with us and tell us his plans. Craig Weatherup and I met him and his agent for dinner at the Plaza Hotel. Before we even got there, Craig and I agreed we were behind him 100 percent. It was a no-brainer. Magic had done great work for us, we admired him, and we didn't see any reason why the relationship shouldn't continue.

I was even more convinced this was the right decision the moment I first shook hands with Magic. He is probably the most charismatic person I have ever met. True, at six feet eight, all he has to do is walk into the room and he has your attention. But beyond that, he has a smile that just fills up the room. Since we had already decided we wanted to keep working with him, we got past the HIV thing pretty quickly and then spent the rest of the evening talking about the future he envisioned and enjoying a great conversation.

I asked him if he had always been a superstar, if he was always that much better than everyone else growing up.

"You know," Magic said, "I learned a lot back when I was in the junior leagues. My team would win, like, eighty to twenty every time, and I would score maybe seventy of those points. But at the end of the game, everyone was always angry. Not just the other team, but my teammates and their parents. I monopolized the ball so much that nobody else got to shoot, so no one was having any fun.

"I realized that I was going to have to get more people involved or no one was ever going to like me. That was when I decided I was going to learn how to become a great passer. We still won eighty to twenty, but I'd only score maybe twenty points and the rest of the team would score the rest. The parents liked me, my teammates were happy, everyone was working together. I had learned how to go from 'me' to 'we.'

"Later," Magic continued, "when I got to the Lakers, I told my teammate Byron Scott that I was going to help take him to another level, that he was going to make the All-Star team, and he did. I told Kareem Abdul-Jabbar that he was going to score more points than anyone in NBA history because I was going to throw him the passes that would get him there. When Kareem broke the record in 1984 by scoring point number 31, 420, the first thing he did was come over and give me a hug and tell me, 'I owe this to you.'"

That really drove home to me this whole idea of synergy, of one plus one equaling three. If everyone knew his role and fulfilled it to the best of his abilities, then the whole would invariably be greater than the sum of its parts.

The Truth Is in the Middle

One of the things you always hear about sports is that a team is never as good as they look when they're doing great and never as bad as they look when they're doing badly.

I think the same thing can be said about individuals. There have been times, like my first Super Bowl ad campaign at Pepsi, when I have been jerked back and forth so fast between emotional highs and lows, I didn't know if I was coming or going.

Super Bowls were always a big thing at Pepsi—very visible, very competitive, the kind of thing that Pepsi loved. As my entrée into the Super Bowl sweepstakes, our ad agency, BBDO, came up with this great theme for a Diet Pepsi commercial. Ray Charles was going to play the piano and sing "You got the right one, baby." But as he was singing it, he added "uh-huh" to the end of the tagline— "You got the right one baby, uh-huh." That "uh-huh" really got my attention. As soon as I heard it I knew it had the potential to be solid gold.

I wanted to make "uh-huh" the talk around the water cooler on the Monday after the Super Bowl, so we came up with this idea that anyone who called an 800 number that we would flash on the screen during the Super Bowl and said "You got the right one, baby, uh-huh" would get a free two-liter bottle of Diet Pepsi.

The ad agency created these four phenomenal commercials—all with Ray Charles surrounded by people from around the world singing "You got the right one, baby, uh-huh." We presented it to the bottlers, who were going to have to stock the two-liter bottles, and they loved it. They gave us a standing ovation. Now I was a genius, a big hero.

Three days before the Super Bowl, I got a call from the Federal Communications Commission. They were concerned that the call-in response to the promotion would be so great it would overwhelm our national telecommunications system and shut it down, including 911 calls. This was also during the Gulf War in 1991, so there was some concern about national security as well.

The next day I went to Washington to meet with the FCC. I walked into the office and there were about twenty people there, all wearing dark suits, and they didn't look like a fun bunch. They wanted to launch right into a discussion about the problem, but I said, "Wait a minute, you haven't even seen the commercials yet. At least let me show them to you." They laughed like crazy when they saw them, but then they got all serious again. "The better the commercials," someone said, "the bigger our problem."

After much debate, we came up with what I thought was a reasonable compromise. Rather than say, "Call this number," we would say, "Go to the ad in your local newspaper to get the number to call." Now it was a two-step process, which would deter enough people to cut down on the number of calls.

I thought the whole matter was solved, but then, at about 9 P.M. that night, I got a call from a woman at the office of the FCC chairman. She told me, "If we encounter any problems whatsoever, you have to be prepared to pull your commercials from the Super Bowl."

"Wait a minute," I said. "I thought we had an agreement. If you can't give us one hundred percent assurance that we're not going to overwhelm the phone lines, then we're going to change the ads and cancel the promotion." But she insisted that we'd need to be ready to pull the ads.

The last thing we wanted to do was put people's safety at risk, even if it was just a small risk. It wasn't worth it, so we recut the ads and took out the free-two-liter-bottle promotion. Then I had to let the bottlers know that the promotion they had loved so much and had sold into their customers wasn't going to happen. No one was happy and I looked like the biggest idiot in the world.

I went to the Super Bowl in Tampa that year—the

New York Giants versus the Buffalo Bills—feeling like a total jerk. It was not one of my better days. But Monday morning I picked up the newspaper and saw the *USA Today* headline claiming our Diet Pepsi ads won the day. As I recall, consumers had voted us the first, second, and fourth best commercials of the game. I got congratulatory calls all day long, including some from people who had hung me out to dry. Now I was the hero all over again.

What's the moral? All of us are going to experience highs and lows on the emotional bell curve, but the truth lies somewhere in the middle. So don't believe your press notices, especially if they say you just came in first or last.

Arrogance Causes Deafness

One of the easiest traps to fall into when you've earned some success is forgetting to listen. I can't stress enough the essential nature of really hearing what someone has to say even if it is totally contradictory to your own beliefs, and I wish this was a lesson I only had to learn once. But in truth, it's something that I have to constantly remind myself of, and others, to do to this day.

Looking back on the low points in my career (those solar shades, for example), I can almost always pick out a moment or moments when things could have gone a different way, if only I had been open to the questions and criticism of those around me. Do you remember Crystal Pepsi, the clear Pepsi-Cola? *Time* magazine called it one of the one hundred worst new product ideas of the twentieth century. It was my idea and one of my deafest moments.

When I first became head of marketing at Pepsi, both the sugar-cola category and the diet-cola category were declining. There were a lot of alternative beverages coming into play. Snapple was hot, as were all sorts of waters. Clear beverages were really popular. One day I was sitting in my office and thought, "Wow, all these clear beverages are doing so well, why can't we do a clear Pepsi?"

I thought it was the biggest idea I'd ever had, so we worked on the product and took the idea out to some focus groups. The consumers loved it. It was novel. It was from one of the most recognizable brands in the world. It was something I had done successfully many times: bring a unique image or product to a known quantity.

Our first test market was in a town near Denver, Colorado, and the first day Crystal Pepsi came off the line, it was the feature story on *CBS Evening News*. Dan Rather was talking about it. People started sending cases of Crystal Pepsi to other parts of the United States where they couldn't get it yet, like they used to do with Coors beer. This was a big deal, a phenomenon.

My first clue that there might be a problem was when the higher-ups at Pepsi made me go to Don Kendall, the founder of PepsiCo who masterminded the merger with Frito-Lay, to get his permission to launch a new product under the Pepsi name. Don is a mountain of a man who calls things like he sees them, and when I pitched him the idea, he didn't like the notion of changing Pepsi so much. He said, "I don't like it, but if you do . . ."

Then I received some unwanted feedback from the board of the Pepsi-Cola Bottling Association. Of course they had heard about it already from our great test results in Denver. They said to me, "This is a really good idea, David, but there's only one problem. It doesn't taste like Pepsi." And I said, "Well, it's not supposed to taste exactly like Pepsi because it's supposed to be a lighter cola with a lighter taste."

"Yeah," they said, "but you're calling it Pepsi." I answered them with more facts from our market research, but I really wasn't listening. We probably could have changed the taste to position it properly, but I really didn't care to hear about it. I was so convinced I had the real deal, I wasn't interested in other opinions.

We were also in a full-court press to get the new product into stores in time for another major Super Bowl campaign. If you're not listening anyway and you're feeling pressure, then you go stone-cold deaf. I was so caught up in my own convictions and so uninterested in having them challenged, I was like a heat-seeking missile that had already been launched. There was no turning back.

The bottlers actually made okay money from Crystal Pepsi because they had said to me before the launch, "David, this is going to be around for such a short time, we're going to charge more money for it." With all the "premium" waters that preceded it, Crystal Pepsi has the dubious distinction of being the first carbonated beverage introduced with premium pricing. *Saturday Night Live* even did a Crystal Pepsi parody with "crystal gravy" being poured out of a bottle. It was around for about a year before we pulled it off the shelves.

Because I hadn't listened to my critics, I was really out there on a limb by myself when Crystal Pepsi went south. The thing is, despite the fact that I hadn't listened to the bottlers or even to the founder of the company, I didn't get fired. Pepsi is a company that knows you won't get innovation if you don't encourage risk. Sometimes risks don't pay off, but that's just the way it goes. I had taken a risk and it hadn't worked out so well, but I never felt like my job was on the line because of it. (It certainly helped that the product actually made some money thanks to its premium pricing, so it didn't send Pepsi down the tubes.) The worst part really was that even after the product failed, I still thought it could have worked if only I had taken the time to work through the issues. But now I'll never know.

7

The Operator

Getting Out of My Comfort Zone

epsiCo is a great company. It was a great company before I got there, and it was a great company after I left, and it was great to me while I was there. I worked with a lot of fantastic people there, and I learned a lot from them.

I feel like I need to keep saying this because I don't want any of my comments to suggest that Pepsi was anything other than a tremendous experience. From a learning perspective, it's useful to concentrate not only on everything Pepsi did right but on what could have been done differently or better. Besides, with the benefit of hindsight it's pretty easy to be a know-it-all.

I know the one thing that Pepsi absolutely agreed with me on was the dysfunctional organization of the beverage division, because it changed it while I was still there.

When I started at Pepsi, there were five presidents: four regional presidents (east, west, south, and central) and a "president of the presidents," Craig Weatherup. Each president was in charge of making all the decisions for his region because after all, that's what presidents do. But there were too many cooks in the kitchen. There was little coordination and too much regional independence to leverage the scale of a national company. It was as if there were five different companies instead of four divisions of one company.

The problem was obvious every time all the presidents met. Each one was so focused on his own slice that he forgot about the pie, and at these meetings no one would really agree or disagree with anything, because the only thing that really mattered was what was going on in their part of the country. They'd mostly just keep quiet until the meeting was over and then everyone would go off and do his own thing.

Those meetings often felt like a big waste of time, but for me they underscored the value of teamwork. I realized that as a leader, you really have to play on two teams—your own and that of the company—or neither of you is going to get very far.

I knew Craig realized the same thing because pretty soon after I came on board he decided to do away with the five-president system. To make the hierarchy clear to everyone and to get rid of the division mind-set, he established that there would now be only one president, Craig, and two chief operating officers, one for the east and one for the west, who would focus on operations only.

The restructuring opened up an opportunity that I hadn't known I wanted before then. The most obvious person for the COO job in the west was Brenda Barnes, who had been one of the regional presidents at the time and is now CEO of Sara Lee. When she was offered the job, she took it.

I wanted to be the guy in the east. The only problem was, I didn't have any operating experience.

Figure Out "the Offer They Can't Refuse" and Make It

I had come very far, very fast, but up until this point in my career, all my experience had been in marketing. As head of marketing at Pepsi, I had gone as far as I could go. If I wanted to keep moving up, I was going to have to get some experience in other areas of the business as well.

The COO position opened up at the perfect time for me personally because I realized it would be a great way to keep my learning curve from flattening out. I needed to know how products actually got from point A to point B to point C and how you make money as a result. That meant learning things like how our beverages were made, how they were packaged, and how they got from bottlers to stores so that consumers could buy them.

I knew I wasn't the perfect fit for the job. There were plenty of people with experience in operations, but I figured that what I lacked in experience I could make up for in dedication. So I went to Craig and told him I wanted to become the COO of the east. He was open to the idea, but Wayne Calloway had his hesitations. I had pretty well established my reputation as a good marketing guy, and he didn't want to lose someone with my experience. I was told he even went so far as to suggest that if a higher title was what I was looking for, he'd make me president of marketing.

It wasn't the title I was after. It was the opportunity to learn. So I went back to Craig with an offer I hoped he couldn't refuse: Give me the position for sixty days, and if he didn't think I was doing a great job, I would go back and do anything he wanted me to do in marketing, no hard feelings, no questions asked.

Craig respected me well enough to take the risk, which says volumes about him as a leader, and he was able to get Wayne to agree as well. I was taking charge of my career, and I think they both respected that. I took the COO job and never looked back.

The Answer Is in the Building

It's funny how when you need to learn something, you absorb it like a sponge, and when you don't, you don't.

When I was Pepsi's chief marketing officer, I must have visited bottling plants at least twenty times. I'd always nod as though I understood what someone was telling me, but I had only surface knowledge of what was going on there because it wasn't my focus. I have to admit, the information would sometimes just bounce off of me like I was wearing an invisible shield because my head was into marketing, not operations.

After I took the COO job, I decided that I had to get help from the people who really knew what they were doing. I surrounded myself with the best operators, people who knew the bottling processes and how to drive sales and profits. I'd get up at five in the morning and have a roundtable with the route salesmen before they went out. I'd ask them: "What are we hearing from our customers? What are we doing well? What do we need to do better?" Then I would just listen. Then I would go out on sales calls with them to talk with the customers and ask them the same questions. Then I would go talk to the guys on the line in the bottling plants and ask them. One of the things I learned, for instance, was that our forecasting process was terrible. We were constantly running out of stock and we weren't getting stuff out of the warehouse fast enough. At the end of the day, I would meet with the marketing unit manager who ran the plant, and he'd ask me how it was going.

"Well," I'd say, "we need to have a better forecasting process. It takes too long to get our trucks out, so we need to look at the loading procedure. Our customers want night-delivery service, so we have to figure that out."

He would look at me and say, "How'd you know all this?"

I'd say, "Well, I asked."

As COO, I was now in a position to make things happen. To this day, I wouldn't know all the ins and outs of how to run a bottling plant, but I could go back to our Pepsi headquarters in Somers, New York, and bring some very impressive resources to bear in terms of both brainpower and financial power to solve the problems at hand.

There are two key things I learned, or at least had reinforced for me, during my first few months as Pepsi's chief operating officer. The first was, focus on the things that matter. I have been fortunate to the extent that I have always gone into a new job in something of a turnaround situation. In cases like that the first thing most people want to do is make some kind of immediate impact, so they tend to gravitate toward the visible stuff like a new advertising campaign or a big new sales promotion. What I learned, however, is that first you need to get the fundamentals right, like how to get the trucks out of the warehouse and how to make sure there's enough product on the trucks when they leave. New marketing initiatives are sexy, but if you don't have the nuts and bolts of operations in place and the machinery humming along, then you're not going to drive more sales and make any more money.

The second thing I learned is that all the answers are in the building. Every company is filled with experts. If you want to learn the company's history, have a meeting with a twenty-five-year veteran. If you want to know what customers are thinking, talk to the people who answer the 800-number calls. If you want to know why the trucks aren't getting out on time, a route salesman who's been at the job for a while is likely to know the answer.

It's like the best major league pitchers and a baseball. Pitchers like Roger Clemens know everything anyone could ever want to know about how to throw that baseball—like if you move a finger a quarter of an inch, or put it on the seam, or if you apply more pressure with a certain finger, the ball is going to break differently. You have that same type of expertise at your fingertips in almost any company. All you have to do is tap it.

This applies to every kind of issue both big and little. Like a lot of people of my generation, I am less than a whiz with technology. Recently, there was some information I accidentally deleted and I was driving myself and Donna Hughes, my administrative assistant, crazy trying to recover it. We finally sent for our head of IT, who first confirmed that the information I was looking for was gone forever, then showed me how to not do it again. Admittedly, this was using an elephant gun to kill an ant, which you get to do from time to time if you're the CEO, but I'm including this story here because with technology, the line between ignorance and expertise is so clearly drawn. In most companies it works like that with almost any pertinent body of knowledge.

Always Ask Questions

I always tell people that the best thing about being new is that you have carte blanche to ask a ton of questions. (My favorite is "What would you do if you had my job?") The trick is to be secure enough to keep asking questions after you've been in the job for a while, when some people might be thinking that you should already know the answers. Asking questions is actually a great way to let people know that they're needed and that you value what they have to say. And I've learned time and again: the most powerful way to motivate someone is to listen to them.

I regularly go down to our lunchroom, see someone sitting alone, and ask if I can join him or her. Once that person gets past the initial surprise and we get to talking, there is no way I am not going to learn something that I didn't know before I got there. Just recently I sat with a young marketing person who gave me some good ideas about how to train new employees based on his own recent experience of being the new guy in the company. But even if I don't get any new ideas, it's a great way for me to take the company's temperature and find out how people feel about where we are and what we're doing. Besides, you never learn much of anything by eating alone.

"I'll Be Back"

No matter how far up the ladder you climb, you never out-grow the need to be challenged, to have someone believe in you and tell you "You can do this." Sometimes the best thing you can do to help people succeed is nothing at all, just stand back and give them a chance to prove themselves. This is a lesson I learned from one visit to the Pepsi bot-tling plant in Baltimore. At the time, the plant was known as "Fort Apache," because it's in a very tough part of town. When I first went there, the Pepsi sign was scarred with bullet holes, and there was graffiti all over the building.

When I walked into Fort Apache, the first thing I did was hold a meeting with a group of employees from sales and manufacturing. I introduced myself, and then asked them straight out, "What's working and what needs to be fixed?" Their answer was "Nothing and everything."

They weren't used to having executives ask for their opinions, but when I asked them to elaborate, I quickly found out that they had plenty to say. It took two hours for them to tell me what was wrong. "It takes the trucks forever to get out of here." "The fountain guys don't get the equipment they need." "The place is filthy." "So-and-so is getting paid more than I am." It was a real air-ing of dirty laundry.

Finally, this one man—he was in the union, so he knew he could get right in my face—said to me, "Okay, you don't seem like such a bad guy. What are you going to do about all this?"

I told him, "I'm not going to do a damn thing." They

looked at me like I was crazy, and I said, "The only thing I'm going to do is come back in six months. You know the problems better than anyone, so you should know the best way to fix them. When I come back, you're going to show me what you've done."

Then I asked them to get me Rod Gordon, the plant manager. In front of all of them, I said, "Rod, these guys have a lot of good ideas, and I want you to work with them. Right now this place is unacceptable, and we have way too much talent around here not to make it work. I'm coming back in six months to see the progress, and when I do, I want to see all the exact same people who are here now in this same room."

The day I came back was one of the greatest days of my life. The workers practically poured out the front door to greet me. They couldn't wait to show me all the improvements they had made. The place wasn't perfect, but it was much better than it had been. They were especially pleased to show me the changes they had implemented to make the truck-loading process more efficient. I was so proud because they were so proud of what they had accomplished. It was clear to me that leading isn't just about taking the lead yourself. It's about inspiring others to take the lead as well.

Get Out of Your Own Way

I had hated giving presentations, ever since that first one I ever had to give, to Rockwell Power Tools, when I was so nervous I ended practically every sentence with a self-conscious "you know?" I hated giving speeches even more. I'd read all my speeches either off a piece of paper or off a TelePrompTer, which was even worse.

You know how they say to start with a joke? Well, I've never been able to tell a joke. I'd read a joke off the TelePrompTer, and then there'd be this awkward silence and I'd want to crawl under the floor. Or I'd mispronounce a word—I could hear myself doing it—and I'd keep reading, but my mind would get stuck on "Oh, no. I just botched that word."

The problem, as usual, was that I was trying too hard and, as a result, I wasn't being myself. This started to change somewhat when I first got to Pizza Hut and we set up the interview format with the David Hartman look-alike. It was impossible for me to read from notes in that format, and I realized how I could make my natural effusiveness work for me.

When I first joined Pepsi-Cola, we weren't doing so well. We had issues with our forecasting, our pricing, our loading process, our delivery service. Practically everything to do with operations needed improvement. In fact, we would have been doing better if we had put all our money into a passbook savings account and earned simple interest on it. I learned that we were going to have a meeting of the entire company, more than six thousand people, at the Dallas Convention Center to discuss the problems, and that I would be one of the speakers.

I worked with Jack Mcalinden, a professional speech coach, to get ready. He taught me a lot, but in a nutshell, he made me aware that giving a speech is like being interviewed on television, which is a kind of hyper-reality. It's theatrical. It's a performance. And you have to get across your sound bites.

Jack taped me giving my speech, and then he said, "You're going to be in front of six thousand people in this giant auditorium. You're a big guy"—I'm six feet one—"so I want you to be big out there. Throw out your arms and move around the stage. And don't worry so much about every word. Get out of yourself; get out of your own way."

He also talked about being dramatic, about using short sentences, about lowering and raising my voice, and so on.

One of the best self-help books ever written is *The Power of Positive Thinking* by Norman Vincent Peale, and it was published more than fifty years ago. Some people have been successful motivating with fear and getting results through intimidation. But for long-term results, there is no doubt in my mind that people respond better to positive reinforcement, to affirmative, upbeat motivation, to "Go, team, we can do this!" This convention was the perfect forum for this kind of motivation because the meeting was largely about pain—customer pain, employee pain, financial pain. All anyone seemed to be talking about was all the things that had been going wrong for us.

I was the after-dinner speaker. I got up there and for the first ten seconds I said nothing; there was absolute silence. Then I said, "There's one thing I want you to know. This is one great company, and I don't want anyone here to forget it." The place exploded.

Ever since the Ray Charles "You got the right one, baby" commercial, I had become known around the company as "the Uh-Huh Guy." I said something else, and a few people responded, "Uh-huh." Then I said something else and the whole convention, six thousand people, turned into an old-fashioned tent revival meeting. To this day, I can't tell you how it happened, but I'd say, "And then we're going to do this," and they'd all say, "Uh-huh," and then I'd say, "And then we're going to do that," and they'd all say, "Uh-huh."

It was one of the most incredible moments of my business career. We came out of our slump shortly after that, and I'd like to think that speech put a little fire in our bellies.

Get Rid of "I Remember When" and Create New Memories

At Yum! we are very big on rituals. We are always bring-ing in our high performers to reward them in some way, and we are always looking for reasons to celebrate.

Before I got to Pepsi, management had bought back a lot of the bottling plants from franchisees. I'd walk around some of these plants and see a wall of Employee of the Month photos, but they ended in 1988, the year Pepsi bought the plant. All the high-touch things that had given the place a sense of community had gone away. Employees would say, "I remember when Bill Smith ran this place. We always had annual picnics." Or "I remember when we'd get rewards for good work." Or "I remember when Bill would come down and have lunch with us." The problem with the Pepsi ownership was that they would bring in professional managers who would live in the community for two years or so and then move on. There was no continuity, no commitment to creating a sense of place.

One of the worst things to afflict a company is this I-remember-when syndrome. It's part of a leader's job to create new memories every day. For example, we started celebrating China Appreciation Week after we opened up our one thousandth restaurant in that country. And when we reached investor grade, we had a big celebration and took a picture of our entire team out in front of our restaurant support center doing a Yum! cheer. We had the picture framed and hung it in our hallway. In fact, we hang up pictures of all our big events and memorable moments so that everyone will remember them.

Lately there's been a lot of research coming out, showing families that actively celebrate holidays, families that do a lot together, are happier than those that don't. And I figure, what works for families can work for companies as well.

Things Aren't Always What They Seem

Most people who succeed in business—whether accidentally or not—look forward to and even worry a bit about where they are going. Sometimes, however, you can read too much into situations and worry too much about making the right impression along the way. There is a difference between looking ahead and looking too far ahead. That's why Wayne Calloway reminded me to keep my focus on the job at hand when I decided I had to be president of something by the time I was forty.

You have to keep things in perspective and not get so

carried away with where you want to go that you don't see what's happening in the moment. Put another way, ambition can cause blind spots. That's what happened to me at one of the first big Pepsi meetings I ever went to. It was in Pebble Beach, California. After I arrived I got a handwritten invitation that said, "Wayne Calloway, Chairman of PepsiCo, would like you to join him for dinner tomorrow night to celebrate PepsiCo's success."

I said to Wendy, "Man, I've really made it. I know Wayne really likes me, but this just proves it."

When Wendy and I arrived the next night, we were seated at table 122, about half a mile from the dais. All the executives had gotten the same handwritten invitation. I should have known.

One time I received an invitation to a surprise fiftieth-birthday party for Joe McCann. Joe was senior VP of public affairs for all of PepsiCo, so I knew all the top executives from the chairman on down were going to be there. I also distinctly remember getting the invitation because it was around the same time as my fortieth birthday.

The invitation said to get there at least a half hour early so as not to spoil the surprise. So, we were getting ready and Wendy seemed to be taking forever. I have a type-A personality anyway, so I was starting to get very uptight. Then Wendy got some makeup in her eye and I started to go berserk. I was trying to be helpful, but I was so worried all I could do was make it worse.

When we finally got to the estate where the party was being held, all the cars were already parked and the driveway was lined with limousines. I figured maybe we could slip in a side door and no one would notice.

Then, all of a sudden, I saw this limo pull in to the driveway and I absolutely knew it was Joe McCann and we were about to ruin the whole surprise. So I literally pushed Wendy into the bushes and jumped in behind her. It was like a scene out of a slapstick comedy, but I was pretty sure Joe hadn't seen us.

When I came through the door, I was at the bottom of a staircase packed with people. All of a sudden, everyone yelled "Happy birthday!" and my daughter, Ashley, came running up to me and said "Happy fortieth birthday, Daddy!" Wendy had set up the whole thing. And I'd been so worried about being late and how my colleagues would look at me because of it, I almost forgot that parties are supposed to be fun. Wendy's great at reminding me of things like that.

8

What Kind of President
Was I Going to Be?

Being the Real Me

I n 1930, in the midst of the Depression, a forty-year-old
gentleman by the name of Harland Sanders opened a
restaurant, Sanders Court & Café, in the front room of
a gas station in Corbin, Kentucky. The restaurant grew,
added on a motel, burned to the ground, and was built
back up again, this time even bigger. Harland Sanders and
his restaurant became so well known in those parts that the
governor of Kentucky even made him an honorary Kentucky Colonel.

But the business declined when, in the mid-1950s, an
interstate highway bypassed Corbin, and within a matter
of months Colonel Sanders had to shut down the restaurant for good. At the age of sixty-five, when most people
are contemplating retirement, Colonel Sanders found himself virtually broke and living off his $105 monthly Social
Security check.

But Colonel Sanders had an idea. He believed that his
recipe for southern fried chicken was the best ever created,
and he was pretty sure that anyone he could get to taste his
chicken would agree. He decided he would sell his secret

recipe to established restaurants for a piece of the profits. He was, in other words, going to earn royalties from fried chicken.

Which he did, charging a nickel a chicken.

Colonel Sanders may not have had much money, but he was nothing if not resourceful. Now somewhat portly, he decided to dress up the way he thought people might imagine a Kentucky Colonel to look—in a white suit and black bolo tie, with a distinguished white mustache and goatee to complete the effect—before hitting the road to sell his recipe.

Colonel Sanders and his wife, Claudia, in an equally colorful antebellum outfit (both are on display at our Colonel Sanders museum today), drove from town to town throughout Tennessee and Kentucky. At each new town, they would set about discovering which local restaurant was the most popular. Then Colonel Sanders would sneak around the back and check out the kitchen. If it met his standards for cleanliness, he and Claudia would make their grand entrance.

Of course, dressed as they were, all they had to do to make a grand entrance was walk through the front door. Invariably, they would engage the owner, and the next thing you knew, Colonel Sanders would be in the kitchen cooking his chicken.

Colonel Sanders actually had two secrets. One was his legendary blend of eleven herbs and spices, the recipe for which to this day remains locked in a safe in our headquarters in Louisville, Kentucky. (Only two people know the actual ingredients, and I'm not one of them.) The other was that he fried his chicken in a pressure cooker.

Not only did this produce flakier, moister chicken, it also meant the restaurant could cook the chickens faster.

Then came the coup de grâce. The restaurant owner would taste the chicken, lick his fingers, and say, "Umm, that's good." That's where "Finger-lickin' good" comes from, and that's how he recruited his first franchisees and ultimately created Kentucky Fried Chicken.

Colonel Sanders was famous for being fanatical about quality, and he really walked the talk. Many a franchisee told me that when the Colonel visited, he would always go into the kitchen to test the chicken. If it wasn't good, he'd let you know by raising his cane and knocking pots and pans all over the place (an act he'd punctuate with some flavorful language). But his dedication to turning out a great-tasting product paid off. Less than a decade later, Kentucky Fried Chicken had more than six hundred franchise outlets in the United States, Canada, and England. With little more than guile and shrewdness, Colonel Sanders had transformed himself into every bit as big a brand icon as Betty Crocker, Ronald McDonald, and the Pillsbury Doughboy, each of which cost tens of millions of dollars to create. A millionaire only after the age of seventy-five, Colonel Sanders is one of the great American success stories.

PepsiCo bought Kentucky Fried Chicken, now KFC, in 1986. Under its stewardship, KFC was an up-and-down proposition—mostly down. PepsiCo's fountain business—simply delivering Pepsi syrup to a store—was a huge revenue stream, so part of the thinking was, rather than have to compete with Coke for these accounts, why not just own big brands and guarantee distribution to those restaurants. So KFC joined Taco Bell and Pizza Hut as part of PepsiCo.

In 1994, I was humming along as COO of Pepsi East when I attended a meeting in the Adirondacks of PepsiCo senior executives. At the time, KFC was struggling for its seventh straight year, and during this meeting, the president of KFC had given a less-than-scintillating presentation. I knew something was about to go down.

Not too long after that, I got a phone call from Wayne Calloway, chairman of PepsiCo. He asked me if I'd be interested in becoming president of KFC. I pretended that I needed some time to think it over.

I was so excited that I went home and said to my daughter, "Ashley, guess what! Your dad is going to be a president!"

She said, "Of Pepsi?"

I said, "No, of KFC," and she immediately burst into tears. She knew the news meant we were going to have to move again, and here she was in the middle of the school year in Connecticut. That was a good lesson in thinking about how someone else might feel about what you're going to say before you open your mouth.

Before saying I'd take the job, I did the same thing I did when I was asked to go to Pizza Hut; I took Wendy and Ashley over to the local franchise for dinner. I hadn't been to KFC for a while, and I was surprised by how good the food was. That made me realize that I had plenty to work with, and I said to myself, "I think I can do this." Of course, I would have done it even if the food had been terrible. You don't say no to an opportunity like that when it presents itself.

Wendy was finishing up her master's in social work at Columbia University at the time and couldn't move right away, so I spent that first year commuting between the KFC headquarters in Louisville and Connecticut so Wendy and Ashley could finish out the school year. (Coincidentally, Wendy had grown up in Louisville, and when she first left home, she'd declared that she'd never go back. Luckily, she changed her mind, and we both love living there now.)

After I accepted the job I got a ton of phone calls offering both congratulations and condolences. KFC had been down for so long, many people both in and out of PepsiCo viewed its situation as very tough, almost intractable. They weren't far from wrong. Sales had been flat or negative for as long as anyone could remember. Even more disturbing was that the franchisees, who owned 70 percent of the restaurants, not only hated us, they were suing us.

The dispute was over territorial rights. PepsiCo was saying it had a right to build new company-owned stores anywhere it wanted to, even right down the block from an existing KFC. The franchisees were saying they had at least a mile-and-a-half exclusive area. To make matters worse, the franchisees had the majority of the marketing votes, which meant they controlled everything from advertising to new products, and they often voted as a bloc—against us.

So I inherited a business in decline and a franchise system that was worse than broken. It was open warfare. Still, I would much rather take over a team that is 3–20 than one that was 20–3. (Can you imagine what it must have been like for the UCLA basketball coaches who followed John Wooden?)

The presidency of KFC was another up-and-out kind of job, and in retrospect, I suppose that if I had failed or had attained mediocre results, that probably would have been the end of my career at PepsiCo, and who knows where I'd be today. (You certainly wouldn't be reading this book, because I would have never had the opportunity to write it.) But the possibilities far outweighed the risk. I was so excited—so overflowing with thoughts and ideas and ways that I might make a difference—all I can remember is I couldn't wait to get started and to find out what I was capable of.

Know Yourself

As president of KFC, I got my first company plane. And since I was commuting to Louisville from Connecticut, a two-hour plane trip, I immediately put it to good use.

I don't want to be overly dramatic here, but on my very first flight, it suddenly hit me what I had just gotten myself into. It was both daunting and awesome. KFC had approximately 5,000 restaurants with 100,000 employees, and for better or worse, either directly or indirectly and whether they knew it or not, I was about to have an impact on every one of these people's lives.

You would think that someone whose goal for such a long time had been to be "president of something" would have given more thought to the kind of president he might want to be, but I hadn't. In my defense, I was so immediately involved in the nuts and bolts of the business, the question hadn't much occurred to me until that moment when I first broke through the clouds just north of Louisville in the company plane.

I began to think about the other presidents and top executives I knew at PepsiCo, which was pretty much the only model I had. All of them were more buttoned up, more formal, than me. PepsiCo was filled with smart people. It was essentially the "university" where I received my MBA with plenty of brilliant "professors" to learn from. But as to personal style, I had always been a bit of an odd duck there—the one among the Brooks Brothers power suits with his shirttail sticking out.

Despite its best efforts to be otherwise, PepsiCo had always been more of a top-down company. Among the upper management there was that tendency of maintaining emotional distance, of putting some barriers between you and the people who worked for you so as to better be able to make the tough calls.

That just wasn't me. One of the lessons I had learned years earlier from Jack Byrum, my image coach—"Don't look up, don't look down, always look straight ahead"— had had a profound effect on me. Now that I was the one people would be looking up to as president, it was more important to me than ever that I come across as just a member of the team—albeit the one who ultimately got to make the calls. That's just who I am—positive, upbeat, together we can get it done. I realized at that moment I could never be "President David Novak." I had to be David Novak, who happened to be president. I no longer felt there was some idea of what a president had to be that I had to live up to. That might seem like a small thing, but it was a big deal for me, and it affected everything I did from then on. Today I preach that the first rule of being a great leader is to be yourself.

And what did "being me" translate to? Well, there were a couple of changes I made right away, changes that ended up serving as the core of a new corporate culture that, at the time, I didn't yet know we were creating.

First, I wanted us to take the business seriously but not ourselves. I wanted to develop a relaxed, casual atmosphere, one that would deemphasize titles and hierarchy, one where everyone would work together and, as much as possible, would know everyone else.

Second, and more important, I wanted everyone to have fun. I've had fun every place I have ever been, and this is a very important component of success for me.

Any business, of course, and particularly a publicly traded business, is all about performance. But I don't believe you get the best performance by telling people that they must perform or else. (You want to guarantee a mistake? Tell someone, "Don't make a mistake.") Instead I think what you tell them is "Let's win, let's win as a team, and let's have fun doing it." Work takes too much time not to have fun at it. In his book *Good to Great,* Jim Collins talks a lot about having the right people on the bus, and I can tell you that hiring people who get results and have fun doing it is very important to us.

Obviously, the idea of having fun at work is not one I invented. You hear sports coaches say it all the time—"I want you to have fun out there." And when the winning team is being interviewed, they say, "We had a lot of fun out there." Conversely, I once heard the coach of a struggling team say, "I wish our guys went out to dinner together more often."

As I was writing this chapter, I read something Matt Bryant, a journeyman kicker for the Tampa Bay Buccaneers, said last year. He had just kicked a sixty-two-yard field goal to give Tampa Bay the win, and after the game he said, "Just before, the snap the ball holder turned to me and said the weirdest thing. He said, 'Just have some fun with this.'"

Having fun can sometimes mean behaving in ways that are not too "corporate." For instance, when I'm giving one of my leadership seminars and I'm sensing the group is starting to drag a bit, usually right after lunch, I have them stand up and give the Yum! cheer, which goes like this:

(Raise arms above head at a forty-five-degree angle.) "GIVE ME A Y!"

(Use arms to make a *U*.) "GIVE ME A U!"

(Place hands on shoulders.) "GIVE ME AN M!"

(Hands on shoulders.) "WHAT'S THAT SPELL?"

"YUM!"

"YAAAY!"

I've actually had financial analysts in New York City

get up and give this cheer, usually very reluctantly, at eight o'clock in the morning. It is followed by begrudging, I-can't-believe-I-just-did-that laughter, but laughter nevertheless. Then I say, "That was just to prove that even finance people can have some fun." (By the way, it's a lot more fun to do the Yum! cheer when the stock is up, but it's really more important to do it when it's down. In fact, people watch the leader much more closely during bad times because that's when they discover what you really stand for.)

Also, when we started to rapidly expand internationally, I had people tell me that our culture would never work overseas—that the Brits were too cynical, the Asians too deferential, blah blah blah. What a bunch of malarkey. I have a picture in my office of about two thousand of our restaurant general managers on the Great Wall of China giving the Yum! cheer.

Fun Can also Be Serious Business

Not only do we try to have fun internally, we try to create a fun, lighthearted image for our restaurants as well. At Yum! I am constantly challenging our team to use humor to break through the clutter and create buzz for our brands.

But having fun can be a serious business. Just look at the fun that advertisers have with their Super Bowl ads each year, but those ads can cost $2 million for a thirty-second spot, and that's just to buy the time. So while a Super Bowl commercial might use humor to grab your attention, it also better be memorable and sell the product.

Even before we were spun off from PepsiCo, our people saw the power of buzz marketing. Taco Bell's April Fool's Day joke of claiming to buy the Liberty Bell and rename it the "Taco Liberty Bell" even gave President Clinton, who was in office at the time, a good laugh. He replied, "What's next, the Lincoln-Ford-Mercury Memorial?!"

What we try to do whenever possible is attach ourselves in a humorous way to an existing news event. That's a lot easier than trying to create product news from scratch. When Pizza Hut, for instance, introduced its new logo, we put one on the international space station and then delivered the first pizza to outer space. When the Rover landed on Mars, Long John Silver's introduced its Giant Shrimp by offering to give free samples to every person in America if NASA actually found water. Our tagline was "One small step for man, one giant leap for seafood." To promote its Famous Bowls, KFC even offered an *American Idol* contestant—who was known more for his wacky hairstyles than his singing ability—a lifetime supply if he dared to show up with a "bowl" haircut.

Even if there's no news event to tie-in to, with a little creativity, you can still use humor to drive sales. Taco Bell, for instance, in order to promote its improved speed of service, convinced Dale Earnhardt Jr. to hold a "speed dating" contest at one of its restaurants. When we updated the KFC logo, we placed a replica in the desert that was so big you could literally see it from space. In each of these cases, the publicity that was generated was beyond expectation.

Of course, if you are going to use humor, you still have to make sure it sells the product. I'm asked all the time about what ever happened to Taco Bell's chihuahua. Well, the chihuahua generated tremendous advertising awareness, but sales actually went down. So we had to fire the chihuahua!

Walk the Talk

"Walk the talk" is such a familiar term today it has lost much of its meaning. This was less so over a decade ago during my early days at KFC when someone left a book on my desk called *Walk the Talk . . . and Get the Results You Want* by Eric Harvey and Al Lucia. I read it and since then it's required reading for everyone who attends my leadership program.

Like *The One Minute Manager* and *Who Moved My Cheese? Walk the Talk* is written in the form of a parable, and it opens with a new president practicing his first speech, which happens to be overheard by the janitor, Clarence. He asks Clarence what he thinks of the speech, and to paraphrase, Clarence says, "Good words, but that's all they are—words—and I've heard them all before. You've got to walk the talk. People don't judge you by your intentions, they judge you by your actions." Clarence then takes the president on a tour of the company and shows him essentially how the road to failure is paved with good, but often abandoned, intentions and that the real gold—the real value—in any organization is the people like Clarence—if they are given a voice.

This really struck home because on one of my first visits to KFC headquarters I was doing a little management-by-walking-around and I said to someone who'd been working there for a while, "I know I'm the new kid on the block, but I don't get much of a sense of what our values are here, of how we define ourselves as a company."

"What do you mean?" he said. "Our values are hanging on almost every wall in this place."

He was right. There were laminated signs on the walls about customer service, about how much we believe in our people, and so on. But I didn't think anyone was really buying into it.

So I did a little investigating. What I discovered was that there was actually a guy who went into his office, came up with a list of KFC values on his own, and then had them laminated and hung up on the walls. And that was it! That's as far as it went. I'm sure some of these things found their way into the policy manuals, but there was not a single program in place to teach these values or to make believers out of anyone. Here we were almost the perfect example of what Clarence was talking about!

The lessons here are pretty obvious, but I came away with a deeper understanding of the need to empower every person in the organization, especially the Clarences of the world. And, of course, just saying it was going to get me absolutely nowhere. The trick was going to be how to put real teeth into these beliefs.

The President Casts a Big Shadow

When I first got to Pizza Hut, my dad came to visit me and I introduced him to the president, Steve Reinemund. My dad said, "Very nice to meet you, Mr. Reinemund."

I was a little taken aback by that, and when I got a moment I pulled my dad aside and said, "You're at least twenty years older than Steve. Why did you call him Mr. Reinemund?"

"Well," my dad said, "he's the president, isn't he?"

That was my first awareness of the size of the shadow cast by the president of the company. Every day I would be affecting in some small or big way the lives of thousands of people. What I began to realize is that everything the president or the leader does is interpreted on two levels. One is what he is actually doing; the other is what it symbolizes.

If I was going to walk the talk, not only did I need to practice what I preached, I had to practice it more diligently than anyone else. If I was having a bad day, I was going to have to learn to expose it to as few people as possible. And if I was going to have an immediate impact, I was going to have to figure out what specific actions were going to send the loudest message. Fortunately, the opportunity presented itself right away.

KFC's Louisville headquarters (which, in the spirit of what I was trying to do, we soon changed to a "restaurant-support center") was located in a big antebellum-style mansion. It was built by the onetime president of KFC and later governor of Kentucky John Y. Brown (who would marry former Miss America, Phyllis George) to look like the White House. Folklore has it that Governor Brown had presidential aspirations and he wanted to try it on for size. Not too inappropriately, it was often referred to at KFC as "the White House."

On the inside as well, it looked kind of like what the White House in Washington, D.C., looks like. It was filled with expensive antiques, and the walls were covered with original paintings, mostly Kentucky landscapes. I felt like I was working in a museum.

So one of the first things I did was get rid of most of the antique furniture and the artwork. I put up pictures of our people all over the place. We also created the Walk of Leaders, which is a hallway filled with a pictorial history of our brands and photos of people we have recognized for great performance. I covered my own office walls with pictures but instead of the usual poses with celebrities or politicians, these were pictures of me with people I've given awards to, or me with a group of restaurant general managers, or me with one of our area coaches, or me with my arm around a dishwasher in one of the restaurants. And when I ran out of space on my walls, I started putting the pictures on my ceiling. You get the picture. We decorated our building with images of what mattered most to us—our people.

Of course sometimes the long shadow cast by the presidency can work against you. Both at KFC and later at Yum! I have done everything in my power to encourage a frank, open atmosphere and to take the intimidation factor out of the presidency. Yet, I have to be ever vigilant to be sure that people are telling me what they really think rather than what they think I want to hear. If people's first thought is "What does David think?" or "What does David want to hear?" then we're sunk.

Sometimes I also feel like I'm unwittingly caught up in the middle of that parlor game "telephone"—where, after a message of mine is passed through several people, any resemblance between what I actually said and what people think I said is purely coincidental. The first time we brought in all our KFC store managers for a national meeting in Louisville, I wanted to show our appreciation for a great year by presenting each of them with a one-hundred-dollar gift certificate. Two weeks later I learned that my idea for the gift certificate had somehow evolved into a ballpoint pen with the KFC logo on it. I quickly reversed that direction and we gave out the hundred-dollar certificates.

One day back when I was still with Pepsi, I was invited to have lunch with Wayne Calloway in his office. It was a beautiful day and as we looked out the window overlooking PepsiCo's beautifully landscaped grounds and magnificent sculpture gardens, I asked, "What is it like to be chairman of a company like this?"

"Well, David," he said, "you always have to be very careful about what you say. One day I was looking out this window and happened to mention that the grass around the edges of the lawn was looking a little brown. The next day I looked out the window and the entire grounds had been plowed up!"

I could spend the rest of the book talking about ways that leaders at any level cast a shadow over those they lead. The president has the power to make or break careers, and I've been aware of this from the moment I set foot in the president's office. People often say it's a privilege to meet the leader, but I believe it's a privilege to *be* the leader.

Reward and Recognize, Part 2

While I was COO of Pepsi East, I was holding a round-table sales meeting early one morning at our St. Louis plant. There were ten or so route salesmen there, and when I asked a question about merchandising someone said, "Ask Bob about that. He really knows how to paint the store Pepsi." Someone else said, "Yeah, Bob showed me more in one afternoon than I learned my first year." And so on around the room: "Bob showed me this," "Bob showed me that," "Bob knows all about that." I looked over at Bob, who was a route salesman like everyone else in the room, and saw tears streaming down his face. "You know," Bob said, "I've been at this company for forty-two years, and I never knew anybody felt that way about me."

Forty-two years and completely unappreciated and overlooked. At Pizza Hut I had seen the positive effect of the Traveling Pan and the Million-Dollar Manager coats, but it wasn't until that morning in St. Louis that I fully realized the essential, even lifetime significance of constantly recognizing the efforts of the people around you.

Pete Harman, whose mantra was "Always be giving back," was not only Colonel Sanders's very first franchisee, he was also the one who provided the business acumen that allowed the company to evolve and grow. I would later learn that all these smart things I thought I was figuring out about leadership were the mirror image of what Pete had been practicing fifty years earlier.

Pete was a great student of human behavior. He'd sit around just watching his customers and pick up all sorts of things. Pete noticed that people would probably buy a lot more chicken, particularly for Sunday family dinners, if they had an easier way to carry it out. So he came up with the KFC bucket, which, with the possible exception of the Chinese-food container, is surely the most famous take-out container ever invented.

In my third week at KFC, I toured Pete's stores with him. He knew all the people who worked there and recognized every one of them by bragging to me about them. When we went back to his office afterward, he disappeared for a minute and then came back with a pin. This was back when I was still wearing ties to work, and he said to me, "It's good to have you here, David. I know you're going to be great. Here, you need one of these. I've got to ruin your tie."

With that Pete took one of his little Harman Pins, which he would give to his employees to recognize their good work, and stuck it in my tie.

You know what? It made me feel great. It was just this dumb little pin, okay? But that was the whole point. Since most of us go about our days rarely feeling appreciated, it doesn't take much to make an impression. (I have a Yum! pin I give out today when I tour our restaurants.)

I was also a little taken by surprise, which is another thing about recognition that I learned from Pete. When recognition is spontaneous, it has even more of an impact. There's a real power in spontaneity. You don't have to wait for a special event. Find an event every day. I'd much rather catch people by surprise. I love to see the look on their faces.

I hadn't been at KFC that long when I learned that our head of information technology was recognizing people in his department by handing out those floppy rubber chickens you see in old comedy sketches. I liked the idea so much that, in true presidential fashion, I stole it from him! I'd carry some around in my briefcase, and then I'd go up to someone in one of our restaurants, let's say, a cook, and introduce myself. Then I'd say, "The restaurant general manager tells me you're doing a great job, that you're a great team member. I've got to give you one of my floppy chickens." I'd then pull a floppy chicken out of my briefcase, write a personalized message on it, sign it, and number it (I gave away about a hundred a year). Then I'd have someone take a picture of the two of us, and I'd say, "We'll send you a copy, but the next time you're in Louisville, I want you to stop by so we can show you where your picture is hanging in my office." Finally, because you can't eat a rubber chicken, I'd hand the recipient a crisp hundred-dollar bill. The looks on their faces are priceless. But they can't enjoy it any more than I do. As Pete Harman taught me, the getting is in the giving.

When Chuck Grant, a great engineer of ours, passed away, I went to the funeral home and saw his floppy chicken at his side in his coffin. His wife told me that before her husband died, he had said that the one item he wanted placed in his coffin to take with him to eternity was his prized floppy chicken. Of course, she had complied. If that doesn't drive home the power of recognition, nothing will.

9

The Career Maker

Turning the Business Around

I ran KFC for just a little over three years, from 1994 to 1997, but I'm spending a lot of time on it here because, though I obviously didn't know it at the time, I was serving my apprenticeship. A lot of what we practice today at Yum! grew directly out of my tenure at KFC. It was KFC's turnaround under my leadership that pretty much made my career and also put me in the right place at the right time when PepsiCo spun off KFC, Taco Bell, and Pizza Hut.

The job I did at KFC captured the attention of my coworkers and the higher-ups at PepsiCo because it was a really tough challenge. I always tell young people today to ask for the toughest assignment they can get so they can find out what they're capable of and prove it to everyone around them. That's how things worked out for me. In fact, solving one of PepsiCo's biggest problems would lead to the biggest break of my career.

Ignorance Can Be an Asset

One of the big things I had going for me when I first went
to KFC is that I didn't have a clue about the chicken business. I'd had some marketing experience at Pizza Hut, but
I was smart enough to know that all fast-food businesses
aren't alike. I knew I had to ask for help, and more important, I knew I had to listen.

I arrived at KFC on a Monday and learned that the
company had previously scheduled a conference with the
premier franchisees—the best operators in the system—for
Wednesday. All our department heads were saying to me,
"Let's cancel the meeting, since you just got here." I said,
"Oh, no. I can't wait to meet these people." Even if it was
nothing more than me telling the franchisees that I was
looking forward to working with them, I was going to
have that meeting.

I had already heard through the grapevine that the franchisees felt that a lot of people in our company really didn't
like the fried-chicken business, so one of the first things I
said was, "I want you to know one thing: I love Kentucky
Fried Chicken." Then I said, "I don't know this business,
but I'm going to go through the process of learning it. I'm
going to find out what the front lines are thinking, and I'm
going to listen to our customers. Then I'm going to go out
to every one of your regional association meetings and
share with you what I've learned. And then I'm going to
ask you how to fix what's not working, and together we're
going to develop a plan to turn this business around."

I thought it was a pretty good speech, but this was a
tough bunch and I knew they were all sitting there think-

ing, "Yeah, that's all great. Now, what about the territory issue in our contract?"

So I added, "I know there's a contract issue, but we can't fix this business by fighting each other. If we can't work together, there isn't going to be any business left to fight over anyway. I'm not going to even talk about the contract until we fix this business, so don't even bring it up."

That meeting took place at the end of 1994. We started turning the business around in less than a year, in large part because we started working with the franchisees.

Shock the System

I have often thought that career-wise the best thing that ever happened to me was coming up on the marketing side of the business. I've always believed that the marketing principles that apply to consumers also apply to people within an organization and even to individuals themselves, whether they're interviewing for a new job, selling their house, or getting their kid into the right college.

One of these principles, as already noted, is "breaking through the clutter." And one of the more effective ways to break through the clutter is what I call "shocking the system," taking whatever the conventional wisdom or prevailing attitudes are and turning them on their ear.

Giving bonuses and raises outside the usual cycle is one example of what I do to shock the system. In fact, I'm always looking for these sorts of opportunities. That's why I handwrite so many of my memos and directives. You don't expect to get handwritten notes from a CEO or a president (and you certainly don't expect them to be signed with a smiley face, as mine are).

Today at Yum! even our annual reports, which we call our "Customer Mania Reports," are designed to stand out from the crowd, with pullout gatefolds and lots of colorful pictures of happy people. They are also very readable. The best advice I ever got about this was from Warren Buffett, whose Berkshire Hathaway reports are so legendary they've become collector's items. Warren Buffett said to me, "I talk to our owners and potential owners like I would to my sister Bertie. Bertie is very intelligent, but she doesn't know our business, so I start out with a silent 'Dear Bertie,' then I write in plain English what I think she would want to know: Here's where we are; here's where we want to be; here's how you can measure us; and here's how it's going to work for you." I sent one of my reports to Warren for his feedback, and he wrote me back, "Bertie would be proud."

In any event, I saw the deteriorating situation with the franchisees as another opportunity to shock the system. So I announced to everyone in the building: "We've hated franchisees for so long it's killing us. From now on, we love franchisees. We absolutely adore them. We want to work with them, we want to learn from them, and we want them to feel the love. After hating franchisees for so long, why do we love them so much now? Because we don't have a choice."

This wasn't too much of a stretch for me because I actually have tremendous respect for franchisees. They're amazing people. A lot of them started with nothing and ended up as multimillionaires owning as many as five hundred restaurants backed by great organizations. Not only are they on the front lines, they think like entrepreneurs because that's what they are, and we'd have to be crazy not to listen to them.

At one of my first regional meetings, one of the older, crustier franchisees stood up and said, "You better be good, son, because there's been a lot of guys like you come through here."

I was a little bit offended by that, but I also knew where he was coming from. The franchisees had seen plenty of salaried people like myself say and do things that directly affected their livelihood—often negatively—and then move on to their next gig. So one of the things I did to shock the system with the franchisees was to tell them that I wasn't going anywhere until we righted the ship. I was there to see it through.

There were, in total, nine regional franchisee association meetings. I'd tell each of the associations what I had learned so far. Then I'd split them up into groups of seven or eight and tell them to pretend that they were the president of KFC and to come back in an hour and tell me what their priorities were. Very quickly, a pattern started to emerge in their responses: quality, new products, more training for our people. Of course, none of their answers were a surprise because we all pretty much knew what the problems were. But it was much more effective to ask the franchisees what they thought than to simply walk into their meetings and tell them what they needed to do. Then together we developed an action plan for working on these things. Just like that, we went from "me" to "we."

To encourage innovation I created the Chef's Council. It was me and six franchisees, including Eddie Sheldrake, a person who complained so much about our lack of new products that I made him part of the solution. We were all passionate about food, so they'd bring recipes, we'd eat all day, then we'd all go home and take a nap. Our Chunky Chicken Pot Pie came out of one of these tasting sessions. So did our roasted chicken pieces.

What ultimately turned KFC around? The finance people will tell you it was the new products we developed. These items created $125,000 in incremental sales per store. But I always say it was a triumph of human spirit because we only developed those things once we started working together.

The best example of this was the crispy strips. Our R&D people had said we couldn't figure out how to get enough supply to produce the crispy strips and then distribute them nationally. Meanwhile, it seemed everyone and his brother had some kind of chicken strips except us. Can you imagine? There we were, Kentucky Fried Chicken, Chicken Capital USA, the leader of the category, with no chicken strips.

So I found out—this is after I'd been there about four months—that there was this franchisee down in Arkansas who was selling crispy strips and his sales were up 9 percent. I said, "Really? Well, let's go down there and find out how he's doing it." So I sent our marketing and R&D teams down there to meet with this franchisee. He took them to his supplier, and his supplier told them how we could do what they were doing, nationally. We launched the chicken strips, and it ended up being the biggest new product KFC had ever introduced. It was a career maker for me because it started the momentum that turned the business around.

Restaurant chains are all about two things: familiarity and consistency. So for a franchisee to start customizing his product line is a huge no-no. Before I changed the attitude, the franchisee wouldn't have even told us about it, and if we had found out about it on our own, we would have gone down there and squashed this guy like a bug for doing something like that without permission. But we wanted to send a different message. We were trying to create a much more open environment, to encourage innovation rather than trying to kill it. So the crispy strips worked on two levels. First, it was the most successful new recipe we had introduced since the Colonel's original recipe, and second, it was saying to the franchisees that maybe we weren't such bad guys after all. It was a brandnew day.

Pride Is a Great Motivator

When I first got to KFC, we were also having a big problem with our ad agency, Young & Rubicam. The TV campaign airing at the time featured a restaurant manager who would talk about what was going on at KFC in the fictitious town of Lake Edna. It was supposed to be folksy, but instead it was very hokey; on top of that, the imagery was terrible, and the tagline was so bad I can't even remember it. Adding insult to injury, I had been there over a month and no one at the agency had even bothered to call me. Even though by contract, the franchisees had the authority to hire and fire the advertising agency, I was absolutely stunned by that.

So I called the president and told him I was coming to New York to introduce myself. When I got there I said, "Listen, this campaign is so bad that I bet you don't have one person working on our account who wouldn't rather be working on something else. I know you can't be proud of this. I also know you think I can't fire you, but if you don't start working with us and start working with me, I promise you just as sure as I'm standing here, I'll find a way to fire you."

Shortly after that we solved the franchisee contract issue. We gave them the one-and-a-half-mile exclusivity they wanted, and we got the right to hire and fire the advertising agency. The good news is, I didn't have to fire them. I had appealed to their pride and raised the bar, with the result that the same team that had been doing such bad work created one of the best campaigns KFC has ever done. Designed to promote inclusiveness, it was called "Everyone needs a little KFC," and it helped turn around the business.

Own "the Heavy User"

One final thing we did right was to identify and cater more to our heavy users—the biggest consumers of our products. In most retail businesses, and in probably any other type of business, it is much easier to sell more to your heavy user than it is to convert moderate users into heavier ones or nonusers into occasional ones. Catering to the heavy user is about keeping your eye on the ball. Sometimes it's more enticing and more creatively challenging to go after your secondary markets, but if you don't keep your heavy users happy, there aren't going to be any secondary markets. The heavy users are also your missionaries, so you always need to be trying to turn them into even heavier users.

Michael Silverstein, a senior vice president at the Boston Consulting Group, told me a story about how Victoria's Secret visited the homes of some of their heavy users, women between the ages of eighteen and twenty-four, and somehow convinced them to reveal the contents of their lingerie drawers. What they found was that these heavy users wore Victoria's Secret two-sevenths of the time—on Friday and Saturday nights. The other days of the week they found it too uncomfortable—itchiness outweighed sexiness. This led to the creation of Body by Victoria, a line of underwear that emphasizes comfort, which is now over a billion-dollar business.

At KFC, our heaviest users were families, and the more kids they had, the heavier they used. So we put a number of new items on the menus specifically designed to appeal to families, and it bumped up our business by 5 percent.

Two years earlier, when I had attended that PepsiCo management meeting in the Adirondacks, KFC had been the butt of a lot of jokes. Everyone else at PepsiCo had come in flying high and KFC had sort of slinked in through a side door. At the end of that second year, the PepsiCo senior-management meeting was held in Greenbrier, North Carolina. I gave a speech about the KFC turnaround, and we got a standing ovation. We had knocked it out of the park. And we flew in and out of the meeting just like the other highflyers at PepsiCo—in our own helicopter.

Lose the Script

The last time I gave a scripted speech was also the first time I put on the chicken feet.

During my second year at KFC I wanted to bring all of our company restaurant general managers—there were almost two thousand of them—to Louisville to celebrate our remarkable success. We literally closed down the Louisville airport and welcomed them with a brass band. We had also made a video to play on the bus ride from the airport to our facilities, the purpose of which was to welcome them to Louisville and to give them a guided tour, narrated by me, of what they were about to see. We had decided to make the seven-minute video a mini-parody of the David Letterman show and called it "Late Night with David Novak."

It still makes me cringe today. I was reading the opening monologue and the "Top Ten List" off a TelePrompTer, and because I'm not a comedian and no David Letterman the jokes were just one thud after another followed by this very artificial-sounding canned laughter. We still show this tape today at all of my leadership seminars—partially to demonstrate how not to give a speech and partially to illustrate the point about playing to your strengths and being yourself—but because of the cringe factor, I always leave the room.

The only part of the video that worked is when it showed me getting off the bus wearing giant chicken feet. It was a bit risky. I could see the headlines—"KFC Tanks While President Runs Around in Chicken Feet"—accompanied by clips from the video. But I have to say that anything I have ever done naturally in the spirit of fun, however excessive or outrageous, has yet to backfire on me. I just happen to be someone who feels very comfortable wearing chicken feet.

That wasn't the last time I wore chicken feet, but it was the last time I read anything off a TelePrompTer. Today I'll make a few notes right before I speak and then let the spontaneity take over.

There Is Such a Thing as Trying to Do Too Much

Shortly after Wendy and I had gotten engaged, I went to Louisville to meet her parents for the first time. Naturally, she was very anxious to know what kind of impression I'd made, so at the first opportunity, she pulled her mother aside and said, "So, Mom, what do you think?" At that moment they could both hear me trash-talking her two brothers, Jeff and Rick, as I was beating them in basketball.

"Well," my future mother-in-law, Anne, replied, "he's a very loud man."

She was right. I can be a very loud man. Wendy says I'm like a big puppy dog, jumping around, barking, and wagging its tail. Over the years I've learned to curtail my natural enthusiasm when the situation calls for it and—when it serves my purpose—to really play it up. But even when I bring it down a few notches, I'm still what you might call a loquacious individual.

So Wendy knows that when I get very quiet, something is up. And toward the end of my stay at PepsiCo, there were a lot of times when I would get very quiet.

What happened was that PepsiCo's chairman, Roger Enrico (Wayne Calloway's successor), had approached me one day and said that now that we had turned KFC around, he would like me to go over and run Frito-Lay. Frito-Lay was a much bigger and more prestigious division of PepsiCo, but once I put my ego aside, it was pretty easy to say no. I loved the restaurant business a whole lot more than packaged goods, so I politely turned Roger down.

Shortly afterward, Roger asked me to run Pizza Hut. Some time after I had left in 1990, Pizza Hut's business had taken a real nosedive, and, since I knew its operations from the inside out, my return would make a lot of sense.

Once again I said no. I told Roger that I had promised the KFC franchisees I wouldn't be one of those fair-weather, in-and-out presidents. But then I made a counteroffer. I said—and this was my hubris speaking—that I would be willing to run both KFC *and* Pizza Hut. I also asked that Gregg Dedrick, my chief people officer at KFC, join me in taking on the dual responsibility. Gregg knew how I liked to work, and I needed a partner in crime.

That decision pretty well brought us both to our knees. We were constantly going back and forth between Louisville and Dallas. (Pizza Hut had relocated from Wichita to Dallas by that time.) And now we had two management structures, two separate groups of franchisees, two sets of financial meetings, two people-review processes, two operating plans—two of everything. I was too stretched to do a good job at KFC or Pizza Hut, and the pressure was really starting to get to me.

Gregg and I did a lot of our traveling back and forth together, and we became great friends. We bonded in the same way that sports teams or military units often do, as a result of external pressures. Most of the time we could see the humor in our impossible situation and just laugh our way through it. But Gregg could also tell when I was really down. Fortunately he knew what the antidote was for me: being around other people.

We always had different groups of employees in for training, and Gregg would say to me something like, "There's a new bunch of RGMs [restaurant general managers] that just got in. Let's go down to the lunchroom and see if we can learn something from them." Within fifteen minutes, I'd be back on top of the world, talking about how lucky we were to have these people in our company.

I was never really able to get that dual-presidency thing to work. Fortunately I didn't have to. Roger Enrico was about to call me into his office and give me some totally unexpected but not totally unwelcome news.

10

The Big Do-over

Shifting the Playing Field

The announcement by PepsiCo that it would spin off its restaurant group came at just the right time for me. I was in the perfect position to head up the new company—or at least, *I* thought I was. (I still had to convince everyone else of that fact.) All that I had experienced throughout my career—from my early days in advertising to heading up two of PepsiCo's three restaurant brands—seemed to be culminating in this moment. I was about to get the incredible opportunity to use all of that background and everything I had learned along the way to create a whole new, and hopefully even better, kind of company.

It was a very peculiar situation from the outset. Here we were, a completely new, virtually unknown company but one with retail sales of just over twenty billion dollars a year, ownership of three of the best-known brands in the world, and around six hundred thousand employees. Yet, for all intents and purposes, PepsiCo deemed the restaurant division a big underperformer in recent years. I didn't agree that it had to be that way under PepsiCo, but however you look at it, I was being faced with the opportunity of a lifetime. If I played my cards right, I had the chance to preside over what certainly would have to be one of the biggest do-overs in corporate history. Ironically, I came very close to blowing it.

Upstage Your Boss at Your Own Peril

You may recall from chapter 1 that just before Roger Enrico, then chairman and CEO of PepsiCo, chose Andy Pearson to be the first CEO of this new company, I came very close to getting canned. Roger didn't think I was the right man for the very top job, at least not initially, but I knew in my heart that I should run this company. I was even prepared to walk if I had to. When I walked into Roger's office to tell him I wasn't going to accept his initial offer of being a "co-something" with John Antioco, who, as you'll recall, was president of Taco Bell, I was banking on the fact that he had a lot of respect for me and that, because I headed up two of the three brands that were being spun off, it would be hard for him to simply get rid of me. No one is indispensable, but I knew I had some power in my corner.

The first thing Roger said in response was, "I need you to team up with Antioco." He was not one to take no for an answer. I left his office that day knowing that he was not happy. Still, I was confident I could find a way to get what I wanted, which was to be the sole leader of the company, but in the event that I couldn't make that happen, which seemed increasingly likely, I had to propose a backup plan.

I suggested that we find a real standout, someone older who was well known in financial circles, to be the chairman of the company for the first few years to help get it off the ground. I wanted someone who would lend the company immediate credibility and someone I could learn from. Then, when that person retired, I would be in a position to take over. I had a few people in mind who would be perfect for the job.

One of the people I suggested to Roger was Jim O'Neil, who was from our international restaurants division. He'd been around the block and had plenty of financial background. Even better, he was a good friend of Roger's. I thought it was such a good idea, in fact, that I went to see Jim afterward to talk to him about it. Essentially—no, actually— I went behind Roger's back, and when Roger got wind of it, he was furious.

A day later I got a message from Bill Bensel, the head of personnel at PepsiCo, saying he wanted to talk to me. When I called him back he told me straight out, "David, you're going to get fired if you're not careful."

I had already made up my mind what I wanted and there was no going back now, so I said to him: "Bill, if you guys want to fire me, then fire me. That's your call."

I knew I was in really hot water and that if I didn't make peace with Roger right away, this whole thing was going to blow up in my face. So I put together a presentation about what I thought the new company should be, and then I called Roger to set up a meeting.

From his tone I knew Roger was still upset with me, but I convinced him to meet me at his office on Martin Luther King Day. It was eerily quiet when I showed up that afternoon because everyone had the day off. I began by telling Roger how genuinely sorry I was that I had disappointed him. I went on to explain that I really believed there was a better way to do this. All I wanted, I told him, was to make a great company, and I laid out my ideas for the kind of culture I wanted to have, the way I thought the company should be structured, what we should stand for, and what our goals should be. At the end of my presentation I said to him, "Okay, you don't think I can be chairman. I think I can, but I'll accept that I don't know what I don't know. So all I ask is that you give me someone I can learn from. I want someone who is going to help me build a great company." I suggested a couple names, one of whom was Andy Pearson.

Roger warmed up a bit after that, and we went out for dinner. He told me I would not be working for Antioco, *but* I was going to have a chairman to work under and he was going to pick him.

I went home thinking that not only had I saved my own skin, but that Roger had bought into my ideas on how to build a great company. He also told me how convinced he was that spinning off the restaurants was the right thing to do. He didn't see much synergy between the packaged-goods business and restaurants. And he passionately believed both PepsiCo and the yet-to-be-named new restaurant company would get much better results and drive shareholder value by being focused on one type of business. That gave me even more confidence, because I respect his business acumen so much.

That was in January. In June he still hadn't made a final decision and we were supposed to go on a road show in September to talk to investors about the new company. Roger was really making me sweat. Finally, I went to him and said he had to make a decision. He said, "Okay, I've got a couple of people I think you can work with. One of them is Andy Pearson."

And the rest, as they say, is history.

Rally the Troops

I knew right from the outset that I was going to learn a lot from Andy Pearson. He had been a senior director at McKinsey & Company, then, as president and COO, he had taken PepsiCo from a one-billion to an eight-billion-dollar company. After that, he taught at the Harvard Business School before moving on to work for the leveraged-buyout firm Clayton, Dubilier & Rice. That's where he was when he was asked to be the new chairman and CEO.

Andy was an incredible cut-to-the-chase critical thinker, but he was also tough as nails and his reputation preceded him. In 1980 he had been one of the subjects of probably the most famous article in *Fortune* magazine's history, "The Ten Toughest Bosses to Work for in America." It was one of those distinctions that could really be taken two different ways, but Andy was so proud of it he hung the article up in his office.

Eventually some of Andy would rub off on me and some of me would rub off on him. In fact, in 2001 Andy would be the subject of a profile in *Fast Company* magazine. This article was entitled "Andy Pearson Finds Love."

What we both found initially was a company that was not feeling a whole lot of love. When a company is sold or spun off because it's a "drag on earnings," what its people hear is "We don't want to own you because we don't like you anymore." What's more, PepsiCo had loaded us up with nearly five billion dollars in debt, which gave us a junk-bond balance sheet and negative shareholder equity. There was high anxiety all around. This wasn't what the employees had signed on for. They had signed on to work for a highly regarded, well-established company called PepsiCo. Even I had signed on to work for a company called PepsiCo, where I had thought I would be for the rest of my life.

As Roger Enrico noted when he first offered me the job of "spiritual leader" of the company, I'm pretty good at talking to people and getting them motivated, so that's exactly what I did in the time leading up to the spin-off. I made the rounds, meeting as many employees in as many divisions of the company as I could (particularly at Taco Bell and in our international division, where I'd had virtually no experience at all). I also met the franchisees of each of our brands, and everywhere I went I talked about why we were going to be a great company.

Because I couldn't meet everyone personally, I sent out a letter to all our employees and franchisees. In it, I talked about how much I loved the restaurant business and how having a restaurant-dedicated company was going to be a good thing for all of us. Then I assured everyone that as long as they and the brands performed, people would be keeping their jobs (I knew there was a lot of anxiety about layoffs in the beginning). To add a personal touch, I topped it off with a handwritten note (something I would do more of after that) listing my "Top Reasons Why the New Company Is a Home Run."

I reminded everyone that we owned three of the world's great brands and that decisions would now be made by "restaurant people" who loved the restaurant business, meaning us. I ended by saying that we had the best people in the restaurant business and that we would now come together to create "the ultimate power of one."

We were on our way.

11

Andy and Me

Making One Plus One Equal Three

The implicit deal that Andy Pearson and I had struck with Roger Enrico was that after three years Andy would step down and I would become the new CEO, provided, of course, that I had performed. While there was no doubt in my mind that I could learn a lot from Andy, I still wasn't totally comfortable with how this vice-chairman-to-chairman-in-three-years scenario was going to play out. (Roger hated that vice chairman title, but I had insisted on it as an ongoing reminder that I was the clear successor.)

I knew that my future would be based on my performance and Andy's belief in my ability to lead the company. It was that simple. From that point on Andy and I pretty much lived together—sometimes literally. Andy decided he would commute from Connecticut, but we were having so much fun together that when he was in Louisville, I insisted he stay at my home. In fact, Wendy enjoyed having Andy so much, she ultimately gave him his own wing, and to make him feel at home, she hung a sign on his bedroom door that said ANDY'S ROOM. She knew how much he loved his wife, Joey, and his family, so she placed framed photographs of his grandchildren around the room, and because he missed his poodle, Gabby, she even bought a stuffed poodle and placed it on his bed. Andy loved Wendy, and the feeling was mutual. He quickly became another member of the family. I got the same treatment from Joey when I stayed at the Pearson house in Connecticut.

The beauty is that what started out as an alliance-driven business partnership became one of the most personal and endearing relationships of my life. Andy became my mentor, my advisor, my teacher, my sounding board, my head cheerleader, and my best friend.

What did I learn from Andy, and how did he help me? Before we even opened our doors, Andy called me one day and said, "I've been thinking about the board. How would you like to have Jamie Dimon? He was Sandy Weill's right-hand man at Citigroup, a young guy, and he could give us financial expertise. And what about Massimo Ferragamo? He's young too, from the fashion family, and he knows the retail business cold. These two guys will be with you for a long time."

I said, "Wow, Andy. That would be great."

He continued: "Also, Sidney Kohl from Kohl's Department Stores. He's a good friend and he'd be super at running our audit committee. And how about John Weinberg? He's chairman of Goldman Sachs and a legend. And Bob Holland—he worked for me at McKinsey and used to run Ben & Jerry's ice cream stores. I'm also thinking about Ken Langone, the cofounder of Home Depot, and Jeanette Wagner, vice chairman of Estée Lauder. Also, Enrico tells me we can get Bob Ulrich, the chairman and CEO of Target."

Unbelievable. I knew Andy was well connected, but this was ridiculous. With nine phone calls over the course of two weeks, he had put together the nucleus of what may have been the best board of directors in the history of the world. Can you imagine anyone doing that today in the age of Sarbanes-Oxley and all the public scrutiny board members are now exposed to?

What impressed me most was that Andy not only asked for my opinion, he asked for suggestions. I suggested we add Jackie Trujillo, who is one of our top KFC franchisees, to provide her perspective. He said, "Great, let me meet her." I told him I appreciated him getting me involved. He said, "We're partners." And from that point neither of us ever made a major decision without the other.

Opposites Attract

If there was ever a case of opposites attracting, it was Andy and me, at least from an outside perspective. We seemed like the Odd Couple. He was Felix to my Oscar. He was Mr. Tough and I was Mr. Recognition. As in most things, the truth lay somewhere in the middle, and we learned that we were actually two peas in a pod. We had our differences, but our mutual respect developed into a deep, abiding affection and lasting friendship.

Andy's reputation for toughness was well earned, but by the time he became our CEO, I think he had already started to soften up a bit. While teaching at Harvard, he was also writing articles for the *Harvard Business Review* with titles like

"Muscle-Building the Organization," but later he would tell me that after his first year, the feedback from the students wasn't good. In fact, they said that he was one of the worst teachers. "They said I wasn't teaching," he told me. "They said I was preaching." So he vowed to completely change his approach. One year later he was evaluated by the students as the best teacher in the school. That was Andy.

My first clue that Andy and I might not be as different as we initially seemed was when we met for the first time to talk about how we could work together to build a new company. Roger Enrico had set up the meeting, which took place at Andy's house in Greenwich, Connecticut. One of the first things I asked Andy was "Who are some of the leaders you most admire?" Not surprisingly, Andy cited Bob Crandall of American Airlines, who had the reputation of being a real tough guy. "That's great," I said, "but I have to tell you, my leadership philosophy is a bit different." I went on to tell him about my cheeseheads (my Pizza Hut recognition award) and floppy chickens, about how important I thought it was to recognize our people, to have fun, and to create the kind of culture that makes people want to come into work every day. I talked about how all this stuff really galvanized people and re-sulted in better performance. To drive home my point, I had brought along a book for him to read called *Nuts,* the story of Herb Kelleher and his leadership at Southwest Airlines. Southwest was the best example I could find of the kind of culture I wanted to create, and if we were go-ing to be able to work together, I needed Andy to embrace these principles.

The next time we talked, Andy said to me, "Hey, I read that book you gave me." I was ready for a debate, but he went on to say, "I see where you're coming from and I can support you in this." He didn't even put up a fight. I knew then that there was more to him than Mr. Tough Guy.

Andy and I first got to really know each other when we traveled together doing road shows to raise awareness of our new company among potential investors. That was a real bonding experience, and I was immediately privy to the breadth of his wisdom, ranging from the insightful ("Nothing good ever happens after 9 P.M.") to the utterly pragmatic ("When you need to find a bathroom, look for the water fountains—same plumbing") to the humorous but true ("If you pay people peanuts, you'll get monkeys").

When Andy visited our headquarters in Louisville for the first time, I wanted to show him right away the kind of recognition culture we had already started to build at KFC. We were holding one of our Two Million Dollar celebrations, where we would recognize all the restaurant managers who had generated two million dollars or more in revenue at their stores. These were always great events, complete with a band—our roving recognition band was perfect for such occasions—and we included a welcome for Andy.

When Andy and I drove up he saw hundreds of our employees standing outside cheering for him with the band playing to celebrate his arrival. He absolutely loved it—the energy, the emotion, the enthusiasm. Later he would tell me, "That whole experience was overwhelming. I knew there was something very different going on here."

Expect Performance

As Andy and I spent time with each other over the next couple of years, we began to trade places. For instance, Andy taught me a lot about performance management and made me a much tougher taskmaster. At one of the first meetings we had with our international division, someone presented a bar graph that showed that we'd improved our return on invested capital from 8 percent to 10 percent. Andy just stared at this chart for a minute. Then he turned to me and, in front of everyone in the room, said, "Let's just mark this moment right here as the last time we are ever going to celebrate mediocrity in this company."

Andy was known for saying to people, "What's the so what?" to get them to focus in on and articulate an idea or problem. He'd follow that up with "What's the now what?" to find out what people were doing about their ideas or problems. Once I saw Andy doing this kind of thing—intentionally creating this dynamic tension on behalf of performance—I picked up on it. I knew how to reward performance and I knew how to demand performance, but I admired how Andy knew the subtle distinction between demanding performance and *expecting* it. If you expect performance, people will rise to meet your expectations, sometimes even surprising themselves in the process. (I remember seeing Coach Bob Stoops of the University of Oklahoma on television after his team had just won the Orange Bowl. He was asked if he was surprised by how well his team had played. "Not at all," he said. "We *expect* to play well, we *expect* to win, and we *expect* to win the Orange Bowl because Oklahoma *always* wins the

Orange Bowl." Indeed, Oklahoma *had* always won the Orange Bowl—when they were in it, but they hadn't been in it in six years!)

One day, after Andy had been CEO for a couple of months, he said to me, "There's a powerful human yearning for a certain amount of toughness and discipline." This was the old Andy. Then he added, "But it has to be balanced with a genuine concern for the other person. There's a big difference between being tough and being tough-minded." When I heard that, I did a mental double take. That was when I realized that Andy was actually learning from me too.

If You Think Young, You *Are* Young

I could write a book on all the things I learned from Andy, but the main thing was how to be eighty years young. If you had ever told me that my best friend was going to be someone almost twice my age, I'd have said you were crazy, but I was the one who occasionally had a hard time keeping up with him.

And, man, was he enthusiastic. Andy wasn't the greatest of golfers, but whenever he'd hit a really great shot, he'd shout, "Yeaah!" and pump his fist in the air. And that would just be on the practice tee. I was playing golf with Andy when he made his first hole in one—at the age of seventy-five! I picked him up, put him on my shoulders, and started running around the green while we both yelled. The caddies still talk about it today.

Andy was a lifelong voracious learner. He would power

through three newspapers every morning. I'd hear him on the phone with his grandkids, and he'd be talking about J-Lo or A-Rod or Jay-Z or 50 Cent. He kept up with everything.

Andy helped me to appreciate how precious every moment of life is and how to live it to the fullest. He embodied the idea that this is not a dress rehearsal for real life; this *is* real life. Every morning I thank the good Lord and try to remind myself to be grateful and to appreciate the day. Andy contributed so much to my positive mental outlook. If youth is wasted on the young, it's because by the time we learn to live in the moment, most of those moments have passed us by.

While initially I had some concerns that Andy would stay on beyond his term, he actually turned the reins over to me a year earlier than what we had agreed to, so I became the CEO on January 1, 2000. (Andy remained as chairman until his three-year contract was up in 2001. I took over the chairman title after that but asked him to stay on our board as founding chairman, which he did.) He said to me, "We're creating a great company, and I want to help you to become the best CEO you can be." In fact, he became a personal advisor to a lot of our senior management. He described it as "spending an hour with your golf pro."

In the fall of 2000, Andy and I flew down to Pizza Hut's headquarters in Dallas for our annual Founders' Day celebration. More than a thousand of us assembled in our auditorium. Andy and I kibitzed onstage, teasing each other and giving each other a hard time and generally having a blast, which the audience seemed to enjoy as well. Afterward, it was time to call up our top managers for the year, and I gave them my recognition award—the chattering teeth on legs given to those who "walk the talk." The managers had been singled out for recognition in front of one thousand plus of their peers, and it was a very emotional moment. Afterward, Andy said to me, "You know, I used to make people cry during their performance reviews. Now I see them cry out of gratitude and appreciation."

Andy died in early 2006 at the age of eighty, and I miss him terribly. I had the honor of speaking at his memorial service, and I told the story about how Andy and one of our younger executives were driving to the airport one day when they had a flat tire. Andy jumped out, grabbed the jack, and changed the tire almost before the much younger man could get out of the car. I also talked about how Andy loved food, loved eating in our restaurants, and would attack a Taco Bell burrito like a pit bull.

After talking about all his amazing traits, I said that knowing Andy, he would have wanted me to cut to the chase. So I summed up by saying, "Andy was like a father, a brother, and a best friend to me all wrapped up in one."

12

How We Would Work Together

Setting Expectations

One of my all-time heroes is Jack Welch, and shortly before our launch as a new company, Andy arranged for me to meet him. We went to his offices in Rockefeller Center, and over lunch, after I had furiously scribbled down almost two hours' worth of notes, I asked him one last question: "If you were me, what would be the single most important thing you'd focus on?"

"You know," Jack said, "when I think back to my early GE days, one of the things I wish I had done was talk more about who we wanted to be, what our values were, how we were going to work together, and how we were going to define ourselves as a company. Later we did define ourselves with one word: quality. Everyone could get behind quality. But back then I did a lot of cost cutting without first taking the time to explain what I was trying to do—to give people the larger picture."

Wow. It was like he validated everything I had been thinking about starting a new company. I'd been thinking really hard about what was going to make our company special and how I was going to spread that gospel like wildfire to our people. I loved the idea because it played to my strength. And once I get excited about something, I won't let up until everyone else is excited as well.

Be Careful What You Call Yourself

We inherited four divisions from PepsiCo—Pizza Hut, KFC, Taco Bell, and International—but other than that, we had everything to decide, from whom to hire, to what our pay policy would be, to how we'd be structured, and so on. We didn't even have a name for the company. So one of the first things Andy and I had to decide was what the heck we were going to call ourselves.

We had some consultant come up with a list of options, which were all terrible, so bad, in fact, that I can hardly remember any of them except Amia, which was supposed to mean "friendly." Ick. I wanted a name that would reinforce our culture, so I recommended Smile—Smile Global. But that idea was shot down because it would be too easy for the media to twist it around. If we got a bad earnings report one quarter, you can just picture what the headline would be: "Wall Street Frowned Today When Smile Announced Record Losses." There's proof positive once again that not all my ideas are good!

Lynn Tyson, head of investor relations, had suggested that we use "YUM" as our ticker symbol. It was in the same vein as Southwest Airlines, which has "LUV" as its ticker symbol and uses it in its theme line "Spreading LUV all over Texas."

I liked "YUM" so much I wanted it to be our company name, but Andy thought it might trivialize the company.

He liked it as a ticker symbol, but when it came to the official name, he wanted something more traditional. He was looking for something that denoted "three" for our three great brands. That's when we came up with Tricon, which was supposed to stand for "three icons." Well, no one got it. Tricon sounded more like the name of an industrial dry-cleaning company, which was bad enough, but Tricon Global sounded like an evil conglomerate from a James Bond movie. It just goes to show you that even when you get what you want, things don't always pan out the way you envision them.

So we began life as Tricon Global Restaurants. I hated it but I was stuck with it. (That is, until I found an excuse to change it in 2002 when we acquired Long John Silver's and A&W All American Food. Since we were now five brands instead of three, the "*Tri*" in *Tricon* no longer made sense and we became Yum! Brands, Inc., which is what we're still called today.)

Just before the spin-off, Patricia Sellers of *Fortune* magazine did a story about the new company. She had recently done an article on PepsiCo, and on the cover Roger Enrico was trapped in a Coca-Cola bottle. PepsiCo was obviously not pleased about that, so our new public affairs officer, Jonathan Blum, really went out on a limb when he invited her to write our maiden story. The article itself was quite complimentary, but the title was "Lousy Name, Great Management."

Jonathan came from Taco Bell, and he had been my first official hire. We didn't know each other very well yet when he walked into my office to show me the piece, and he was a little concerned about how I would react to the headline. I looked at it a moment and said, "Well, that's a heck of a lot better than 'Great Name, Lousy Management,'" and we both cracked up. Jonathan later told me that he knew at that moment that things were truly going to be different at this new company and that we were going to have a lot of fun.

Get People Involved from the Get-go

Since my conversation with Jack Welch, I was more convinced than ever that we had to clearly define what our basic message would be. One of the first things we did was create the Partners' Council, which was made up of the presidents and chief operating officers of each division of the company as well as my direct reports, fourteen people in all. I made it our first task to create a vision for the company and to agree on what our values would be. I had learned that getting people involved from the very beginning is much more effective than shutting yourself up in a room and deciding everything on your own. It's simple psychology. People are much more likely to believe in something if they've had a hand in creating it. Someone once said, "No involvement, no commitment," and I couldn't agree more.

To kick things off, I took the first crack at our mission statement: "Be the best restaurant company in the world." Everyone agreed that that didn't quite work. Too simple, maybe. Or too broad. Then someone—I don't even remember who—pointed out that all great companies have a noble cause. We couldn't just say we wanted to be the best for the sake of being the best; we had to offer something that would make people's lives better. That's when we came up with the mission statement that we still rally around today, one that speaks to our desire both to have fun and to serve customers: "To put a yum on customers' faces all around the world."

Simple, easy to remember, to the point. *And* it's an idea that everyone in our company can get behind. Nothing excites an organization more than listening and responding to the voice of the customer.

Create Ownership

In the beginning most of our decisions about what kind of a company we wanted to be had to do with how to keep our employees, at all levels, invested in and excited about the success of the new company. One of the things we learned from looking at other successful companies at the time, such as Home Depot and Citigroup, is that one of the best ways to get people to feel invested in their company is to make them owners, literally.

We thought it was important, too, so we started a program called Yum! Bucks. Through Yum! Bucks, we gave initial stock options to all five thousand of our company restaurant general managers, the people we consider our most important leaders since they are out there on the front lines building the teams that satisfy our customers. To underscore the point, we put a drawing of three of our RGMs on our stock certificate. The initial grant we gave each was for twenty thousand dollars in stock options with the right to earn an additional ten thousand dollars every year through performance. We also required all executives to put a portion of their overall earnings into stock and created a program for them to buy stock at a healthy discount. That meant that the bottom lines of individual employees were intimately tied to the company's bottom line. It was a great incentive for everyone to really care about and feel accountable for where this new company was headed. We wanted as many people as possible to have skin in the game.

Make Big Days Big Events

Our official spin-off day, October 7, 1997, was a great day for us. The Partners' Council and some of our board members flew to New York and had breakfast at the New York Stock Exchange, where Andy and I rang the bell together. Wendy and Ashley and Andy's family stood up there with us, and the NYSE told us it was the first time it had ever allowed family members on the exchange platform. (Who knows if that was true, but it sounded good to me!) Then we went down onto the exchange floor and treated all the traders to pizza, tacos, and chicken. The stock exchange's annual report that year included a picture of Andy and me on the floor—he was wearing his Tricon hat and I was wearing the Pizza Hut cheese head recognition award—and we were handing out floppy chickens and coupons.

Prior to spin-off day, Andy, our CFO, and I went out on a road show—to New York, Boston, Portland, Kansas City, Chicago, Houston, all over the country—to talk to investors and drum up enthusiasm for the new company. Well, it worked. Our stock price on spin-off day came in at thirty dollars, about six dollars more than our investment bankers predicted.

From the stock exchange, we took helicopters to the airport so we could get back home to Louisville in time for another celebration with the rest of the company. It was a picture-perfect day with not a cloud in the sky. As we flew over the Statue of Liberty, I looked at my family sitting next to me and couldn't help but think about my humble beginnings and how far I had come. I was high as a kite.

Back in Louisville we held our first Founders' Day, which we still celebrate each year on October 7. Our employees kicked off the celebration with a parade at the local sports arena, Freedom Hall, to mark our freedom from PepsiCo. Then we had a global meeting via video conference, broadcast to our restaurant general managers all over the country and around the world. No one was left out. Where they couldn't get a live feed in places like Australia, India, and China, we aired the celebration with a time delay or sent out DVDs. Every one of our companies around the world had a Founders' Day celebration that day.

Newswoman Joan Lunden was our master of ceremonies, and we launched the company by talking about our mission statement. I did the Yum! cheer for the first time that day and unveiled my new recognition award—the Yum! walking teeth, which not only symbolizes walking the talk but goes with our mission of putting a Yum! on customers' faces around the world. (The walking teeth is my version of the floppy chicken except that instead of giving away one hundred dollars with it, I give away three hundred, since we have three great brands to celebrate.)

That was a great day for everyone. Not only did we launch Tricon with great success, but a lot of our ideas for making a great company were introduced to our six hundred thousand employees around the world. Looking back on it now, I can see how that day foreshadowed, in so many ways, what our company was about to become.

Think "Duckies and Goats"

When I would read to my daughter, Ashley, when she was a little kid, it always seemed like practically every book was short, to the point, and about duckies and goats, so "duckies and goats" has become my phrase for "keeping it simple."

It's a huge concept for me. It harkens back to when I was working for Tom James at Ketchum learning how to make everything you want to say fit onto one page. So in addition to keeping our mission simple—to put a Yum! on customers' faces around the world—the Partners' Council and I came up with a short list of our primary values to simply communicate to everyone what we believed in and what the company would stand for.

All too often values are just a whole lot of talk and not enough action. So in order to make sure ours really mattered, we studied what behaviors our successful restaurants had in common. We found eight in all. Instead of calling them values, we called them our How We Work Together leadership principles. They were:

1. Customer focus. In successful restaurants, team members always listen and respond to their customers.

2. Belief in people. We want *all* our team members to understand that their contribution is valued.

3. Recognition. We want to reward and recognize those contributions every chance we get and have fun doing it.

4. Coaching and support. All leaders need to be more than just bosses; they need to be invested in the success of those they lead.

5. Accountability. Because results matter.

6. Excellence. All success comes from taking pride in doing a great job.

7. Positive energy. You can feel it when you walk into a place where customers are having a good time and the team is doing a great job.

8. Teamwork. Because we make it happen together.

We introduced these principles to everyone during our Founders' Day celebration as a way to start us all off on the right foot. They are simple, to be sure, but we also back them up with programs that make them real to people (more on those later on).

Go Public

When you go public, you can't go back.

As soon as you say something out loud, people start holding you to it; it's one of the best and simplest methods for motivation that I've ever found. That's why we went public with How We Work Together right off the bat and said we would drive these leadership principles deep around the world. I knew that if we shared them with everyone in the company across the globe, then we'd have no choice but to figure out how to make them work. Either that or we'd end up looking pretty bad, because if you don't do what you say, you lose your credibility to lead. And that makes it really hard for people to believe what you have to say the next time.

We also rolled out our Founding Truths that day. These were the ways in which our new company was going to be different from PepsiCo. We wanted to set ourselves apart, not only to give our company its own identity but because the restaurant brands hadn't done as well as we thought they could have under PepsiCo's stewardship. Our Founding Truths included ideas such as "Run each restaurant like it's our only one," "The RGM is our number-one leader," and "Franchises are vital assets." It was our way of going public with the notion that, unlike PepsiCo, we were going to be a truly restaurant-centric company.

When I first became president of KFC, I told the franchisees I wasn't going to leave until we turned the business around. I said it to get them to trust me because they were so used to having corporate guys come in, work for a couple of years, and then move on, so that there was no sense of continuity, no sense that the president really cared about the company as more than just a stepping-stone in his career. As soon as I said it, however, Gregg Dedrick, my chief people officer at the time, came to me and said, "David, I don't know if you're ready to say that yet."

I said to him, "That's why I'm saying it. If I go public, I'll stick to it."

It worked. We were able to turn the business around, and I kept my word to the franchisees, even after Pepsi offered to make me president of Frito-Lay, a bigger and more lucrative division of the company.

Going public is not only a great motivational tool, it's also a way of demonstrating you mean what you say. From day one, I've tried to make it clear that our expectations for the new company were high, which I hoped would challenge our people to rise to the occasion. If you want to get something done, go on record and tell people you're going to do it. That simple act puts pressure on you to get it done.

I've used the same technique for losing weight, or at least I'm trying to. Every one of our administrative assistants has a candy dish on her desk; one has Twizzlers, another has Iron Mikes, and another has Caramel Nips. A few months ago I realized I was making trips down the hall just so I could eat the candy—and that I had put on about five pounds. So I went public. I went out into the hall and announced to everyone within earshot, which was pretty much the whole floor, "Okay, that's it for me. No more candy for the rest of the year!" I still haven't taken off the pounds, but I've stopped eating the candy.

Make Margaret Mead Proud

I'm no anthropologist, but if I somehow got lost in the middle of a jungle and stumbled upon an undiscovered tribe, I can tell you two things those tribespeople would have in common with one another: a common language and shared experiences. Companies are no different.

Common Language

We've worked hard to develop a language that supports our values. For example, early on I wanted to get people to start thinking differently about their jobs, and that's when we started using the term "coach" instead of "boss" to reinforce the leadership principle of "coaching and support." People often live up (or down) to the title you give them, and coaches are people who are invested in making people better. For that reason, we have area coaches, market coaches, regional coaches, and head coaches, instead of operators, managers, and directors. It's also why we all use first names. No one calls me Mr. Novak for long.

Instead of a corporate headquarters, we have our "restaurant support center." Instead of just division presidents, we have "chief concept officers," and so on. These are the kind of small things that reinforce a very different kind of working environment. Over the years, we've continued to add terms to our shared vocabulary, including "BLAST," "CHAMPS," "the F's," "the Mood Elevator," and so on (I'll talk more about these in the coming chapters).

Shared Experiences

Our Founders' Day was our first shared experience as a new company, which is why we used it as an opportunity to show off many of the principles that would come to define our culture: recognition, fun, teamwork, et cetera. Our employees around the world participated in celebrating those ideals on that day and every October 7 (our company's birthday) since. We've made it an annual event to remind people what we're all about. And we don't stop there. We have leadership seminars, recognition ceremonies, company retreats, spontaneous parties—all sorts of things to get people out of their own little corner of the company and sharing experiences with their coworkers.

Given the recent success of McDonald's, I initiated a global McDonald's immersion day for all our senior teams. Every team spent a full day visiting McDonald's stores and drawing their own conclusions on why they had turned their business around. We shared our key takeaways and now have a common experience to build upon, not to mention some good ideas that will work for us.

As I learned when I was at PepsiCo, each new generation of a company needs to create its own memories. When your employees say, "I remember when . . ." they should not be referring to some previous leadership; they should be referring to last month or last week. Better yet, they should be saying, "Can you believe what we just did?!"

13

Taking People with You

Practicing What You Preach

About six months before the spin-off from PepsiCo, Roger Enrico called me into his office and said, "David, I know you have all these theories about leadership, and they seem to be working. I'd like you to put together a program you can teach our high-potential leaders."

I considered it a real compliment and was thrilled to have the assignment. I worked hard to create a presentation that I hoped would not only inform but inspire and entertain, and I was really looking forward to the opportunity to share some of my ideas with my colleagues at PepsiCo.

I never got the chance. The news that we were being spun off came the week before we had scheduled my first seminar. Since we were no longer going to be part of PepsiCo, I canceled it. So there I was with what I thought would be a great program and no one to give it to.

I didn't want all my hard work to go to waste, so once we got the new company up and running, I began thinking about how to evolve and use my program, which I called Taking People with You, at Yum! Brands. Once again, I harkened back to my first conversation with Jack Welch and decided to use it as a vehicle for getting people to fully understand our vision, strategy, goals, and culture. The reason was simple. Getting people excited about what they are doing, making them feel part of the team, and taking them along for the ride of their lives are the things I do best. Now I would have a chance to give my seminar to our own people who were part of our own new company.

Don't Just Stand There, Teach Something

The first time I presented Taking People with You, my "audience" didn't even fill a conference room. It was a total of eight European general managers in a hotel in London. In the years since, I have presented this talk almost fifty times and to ever-expanding groups, now sometimes up to one hundred people. My goal is to reach everyone in our organization, both here and abroad, from our area-coach level on up, a total of around five thousand people.

The seminar is always evolving, for the better, I hope, and getting tighter. What started out as a three-day seminar is now down to a day and a half. I have also thought about modularizing it so that other people within the company could present it, but I have come to realize that the fact that I personally give it may be more important than the content.

There are two reasons for this. First, it puts a human face on the company and gives people who might not otherwise ever see the CEO the opportunity to spend personal face time with me. That so many people throughout Yum!

now know me and feel comfortable around me is not only important to me, it may be fundamental to our culture.

Second, it sends the subliminal message that "if David, our CEO, devotes so much of his time to this, then all this stuff about teamwork and learning how to be a great leader must be pretty important."

In fact, one question people always ask me is how I can spend so much of my time teaching this program. I tell them that it's the most effective and efficient thing I do because there's nothing like hearing it from the horse's mouth. It really gives people the sense that I am living our values, and that inspires them to do the same.

Besides that, all the participants bring to the seminar the project they are working on that they believe will have the biggest impact on our growth. I get to learn about people's ideas and to coach them on how to develop an action plan to get their ideas accomplished. I always ask people what would happen if we could make their initiatives work, and the answer, inevitably, is more growth for the company. So believe me, these seminars are well worth my time.

Here's the "Cliffs Notes" version of my fifteen lessons for Taking People with You:

First we cover the mind-set.

1. Be yourself. Be genuine because people can see through phonies in an instant.
2. Wipe out "Not invented here." Listen and involve others; learn from the best.
3. Unleash the power of people. No involvement means no commitment.

4. You've got to believe. If you don't see it happening, no one else will either.

Then we cover what you do.

5. Have a plan: Strategy (the what), structure (the tools), culture (the work environment). A road that leads to nowhere is hard to follow.
6. Tell it like it is. As I believe Napoleon said, "The responsibility of the leader is to define reality and create hope."
7. Create a vision and personalize it. People need to say, "I understand it, I'm excited about it, and I can make it happen."
8. Gain alignment every step of the way. Again, no involvement means no commitment. Skip a layer and you will ultimately pay the price.
9. Structure and process enable execution. You can't get things done without the proper resources. If it's important, put process and discipline around it.
10. Make "how we work together" a big idea. Be a team and have fun getting it done.

Then we cover how to keep it alive.

11. Market the change; be bold. Remember, don't be a bad ad, be a good one. (I'll explain this later on.)
12. Measure, coach, and reward the right things. Measure the vitally important. Reward the doers.

13. The change is never over. Be careful to continually reinforce the results you want, and don't move on before you've done the job.

14. Engage in productive conflict. Some people will say every step of the way that it can't be done. Acknowledge that they might be right. Understand why they're saying it. Then follow your convictions.

Last, but not least:

15. Go from me to we. This is *the* job of every leader!

Now, what I really want to cover in this chapter is not the specific content of the seminar, which is sprinkled throughout the book, but why I believe it is important and, even more fundamentally, how I believe we learn.

Reach Out and Touch Someone

I can best demonstrate the importance of reaching out and touching someone by sharing with you how I open the seminar. I ask every participant to think about who their personal business mentors have been and why. I tell them my own business hero was Andy Pearson and give them a few Andy stories to illustrate why. Then we break into groups of about twenty and go around in a circle and have each person talk about the person who has meant the most to him.

The answers I've heard could fill a book. Many people talk about issues of self-esteem or how someone pushed them to be better than they thought they could be. On many occasions I've heard foreign-born workers talk about how a boss made them write down every English word they didn't know and how they learned to speak English fluently as a result.

Next, we reconvene in the larger group and discuss some of the traits that were exhibited by the mentors: integrity, passion, inspiration, a positive outlook, and so on. A lot of people said it was someone who "helped me realize what I could achieve" or "really cared about me as a person."

Then I try to get them to go a little deeper. I say, "Now suppose you were a fly on the wall, looking down on this room ten years from now. What would you like people to be saying about you? How would you feel if someone were saying that you were the person who had the greatest impact on his or her professional life?"

For that one brief instant the look on people's face is priceless. Here they were, a half hour earlier, wondering if they should really be taking time away from their business to attend the session, and now they are so totally lost in their own thoughts they barely know where they are.

These are the moments I live for, when something I have said or done touches people in a way that compels them to examine their innermost selves—when maybe, in some small way, I have made a difference in their lives.

Self-Discovery Is the Key

My leadership program is more of a discussion group and question-and-answer session than it is a one-way presentation. I will ask a question or show a video, and then we'll discuss how what we've just seen might apply to the individual or the organization as a whole. This is based on my deeply held belief that self-discovery is the key to learning, whether it's learning how to do something new or better or learning something about yourself. You can tell the same thing to people a thousand times, but they don't really own it until they discover it for themselves.

This obviously isn't an original insight. Socrates talked about how important it is to "know thyself" several thousand years ago. And the Q&A that I use in my seminar is just my version of the Socratic method—using a series of provocative questions to encourage the listener to think and to come to his or her own conclusions.

I have really pushed the use of this approach within the context of our training. Just the corporate world's use of the word *training* illustrates part of the problem. Training implies a kind of rote monkey-see-monkey-do process as opposed to learning, where the emphasis is placed on engaging and involving the listener.

One example of the latter is a program we instituted for dealing with customer complaints called LAST, which stands for "Listen, Apologize, Satisfy, and Thank." It is taught by our area coaches through a system of role playing so that the team member can empathize with, or at least appreciate, the customer's point of view. Admittedly, more recently, we had to change LAST to BLAST because we were finding that first the server had to *believe* what the customer was saying or everything after that pretty much fell apart. Nobody said this stuff was easy.

As you might guess, employee turnover at the store level is pretty high in our industry, so I'd like to think that even if someone is with us for a very short time that, through our BLAST concept, they leave with some life lessons in conflict resolution. More important, our people are learning how to do a better job of making sure our customers are happy.

As I said in an earlier chapter when discussing "the third idea," what you want to do is plant the seeds by sharing everything you know. The best ideas in a company are the ones that people come up with themselves because then they really own their ideas and are committed to making them work.

Be a Good Ad

One of my keys to taking people with me is applying my marketing background to human relations. Motivating your people to put forth their best effort is really no different from motivating customers to buy your product.

During my seminar another question I ask in the hopes of provoking self-examination is "Are you a good ad or a bad ad?" Then I throw open the floor for discussion about what characteristics make a good advertisement or commercial—it's memorable, engaging, entertaining, focused, sends a clear message, makes you want to see it again, makes you want to buy the product—and what makes a bad ad, which is obviously just the opposite—it's forgettable, insulting, boring, and you don't have a clue what they're selling.

Then I ask, "How many of you have worked your butt off on something and gotten zero credit for it?" You should see how quickly every hand in the room goes up. This leads to "If you didn't feel you got the credit you deserved, was your contribution memorable? Did you engage other people? Were people buying into what you were selling?"

The key to being a good ad is truly understanding your target audience. Ask yourself, Who do I need to influence to take people with me? What are their perceptions, habits, and beliefs? And then develop an action plan that is relevant to the people you need to lead.

Are you a good ad or a bad ad? It's a simple way to get people to take a look not only at what they are contributing but how.

Talk Is Cheap

Not too long ago I came across a value statement from another company in which the values are so noble and well thought out that I've shared it ever since with people in my leadership program. It goes like this:

RESPECT: We treat others as we would like to be treated ourselves. We do not tolerate abusive or disrespectful treatment. INTEGRITY: We work with customers and prospects openly, honestly, and sincerely. COMMUNICATION: We have an obligation to communicate. Here, we take the time to talk with one another . . . and to listen. EXCELLENCE: We are satisfied with nothing less than the very best in everything we do. We will continue to raise the bar for everyone. The great fun here will be for all of us to discover just how good we can really be.

Then I tell everyone what company this value statement came from: Enron, during their time of corruption.

Values aren't something you write down on a piece of paper, then put in a drawer or hang on the wall. Values are something you live by every day. That's why after we came up with our How We Work Together leadership principles, we had to do everything we could to make them real for our people.

When Roger Enrico referred to me as the "spiritual leader" of the company, he meant it, but he also said it to suggest all the things I *didn't* know. While I may have been offended by the context, it was still the highest possible compliment he could have paid me. He saw me as someone who was not only living my values but imparting them to others by example. I try to do that every day. Even if the leaders of Enron didn't know what was going on in their own company, preposterous as it may seem, their failure to live their own values is a betrayal of a far greater magnitude.

To avoid an Enron-type situation with our own values, I knew we needed to train our people and create programs to support and reinforce our values every day. I immediately thought of Larry Senn, founder of Senn Delaney Leadership, LLC.

I first heard of Larry when I received an unsolicited letter from him while I was president of KFC. Having started out as a copywriter, I have a real appreciation for the written word, and this was one of the best pitch letters I have ever seen. It's hard to describe what Larry does, but I guess you could say he is an expert in creating a positive culture by teaching self-awareness. I agreed to meet with him, and I liked what he had to say, so I invited him to lead a team-building seminar with my KFC executive team at a retreat we were having at a resort called Blackberry Farm in Walland, Tennessee.

Much of what Larry taught us that day became part of our training programs at Yum! and, in fact, part of our company language, a kind of internal shorthand for communicating with one another.

One exercise helps show where you are in what Larry calls "the Mood Elevator." His theory is that you make the best decisions when you are in a state of gratitude, which is the top floor, and your worst decisions when you are angry or in a bad mood, which is the bottom floor.

The point of this exercise is to promote positive energy (How We Work Together principle number 7), and I have to say that there is one advantage that I did not foresee. If I'm cranky or moody and if someone doesn't want to confront me about this directly, all that person has to say is, "Where are you on the Mood Elevator today, David?" and I know what he is trying to tell me.

Larry also uses the Accountability Ladder, which is about taking responsibility for your actions (HWWT principle number 5) and getting rid of victim thinking. He taught us an exercise where you play the victim and talk about how you got totally screwed over in a particular situation. Then he flips things on you and asks you to take responsibility for what happened and list the things you could have done to either change or avoid the situation to which you fell victim. I did this exercise with a top level KFC executive who wasn't performing very well as a leader. She was never able to communicate effectively with her team, so they never quite understood what she wanted them to accomplish. They were like a bunch of chickens with their heads cut off, running around without any direction, and as a result, productivity was low and getting worse. In her mind, this was everyone else's fault—until she began listing things she could have done differently. She finally realized that she had no one to blame for her team's failings but herself.

Mind Your F's

Another of Larry's exercises has become very much a part of our culture. "The F's" demonstrates how a simple idea can be used to provoke thought and promote good values in the workplace.

Here's how it works. Read the following statement

carefully and concentrate on counting the total number of F's.

THE MOST EFFECTIVE OF ALL HUMAN FEARS WHICH PREVENT THE DEVELOP-MENT OF FULL POTENTIAL ARE THE FEAR OF FAILURE AND THE FEAR OF SUC-CESS. . . . IT IS A THIEF OF INNOVATION AND OF SATISFACTION. (© Senn Delaney Leadership, LLC)

When I first did this exercise I counted nine F's, which I can tell you is the wrong answer. From the standpoint of self-knowledge, one of the things I learned is that maybe I'm not as sharp as I think I am, or at least as thorough. But what really blew me away was how totally convinced I was that I had the right answer.

What this showed me is that for a passionate person such as myself, maybe I can become so attached to a particular point of view that I fail to consider that there may be other valid points of view as well. The strength of my conviction doesn't necessarily make me any more correct. In fact, it can be a roadblock. (The reason, by the way, that I missed so many F's in the exercise is that, like most people, I overlooked the F's in all the *of*'s because they have a V sound and are the smallest words.)

Larry also pointed out that overlooking the F's can be symbolic: What else might I have overlooked? As a team member, what other contributions or opinions may I be unintentionally (maybe even intentionally) ignoring? Am I paying attention to the small things, to the people with less power? Again, in terms of our culture, asking people if they're "seeing the F's" is a way of pointing this out without being confrontational.

In any event, here is the right answer.

THE MOST EFFECTIVE OF ALL HUMAN FEARS WHICH PREVENT THE DEVELOPMENT OF FULL POTENTIAL ARE THE FEAR OF FAILURE AND THE FEAR OF SUCCESS. . . . IT IS A THIEF OF INNOVATION AND OF SATISFACTION. (© Senn Delaney Leadership, LLC)

Another time, once I knew the right answer, I assumed it was "fifteen" without even bothering to read the statement. But someone had gone and changed it on me. I was wrong again, but this time I learned a different lesson. In business, someone's always changing the rules or pulling the rug out from under you. So you'd better stay on top of your game and see things as they really are rather than as they appear to be or as you would like them to be. Somebody might even change the statement on you!

Learn from Superstars

I believe in that old Chinese proverb "When the student is willing, the teacher appears." But I would add, "It also doesn't hurt to be a little proactive about it."

When we are grappling with a specific challenge, I am much more likely to bring in an accredited expert than I am a consultant. In fact, I think too many executives use management consultants to do the things they should be doing themselves. So when I want some outside help, I usually find an established business figure or the author of a well-received book on a particular subject. Usually these experts are also accomplished speakers, but I'm not interested in hearing their usual stump speech. What I do is bring in as many of our top people as I can, and then we do a Q&A with them.

For instance, we brought in Jim Collins, author of *Good to Great*. Jim came up with the whole concept of "building the clock," or creating a company that, over time, can withstand cultural or personnel changes—including the CEO—and keep on ticking. Jim was a natural when it came to speaking about the keys to building a truly great company and establishing a culture and processes that would outlive even those who established them.

At various times we've also brought in Ken Blanchard, author of *The One Minute Manager;* Larry Bossidy, coauthor of *Execution: The Discipline of Getting Things Done;* Howard Schultz, the founder of Starbucks who wrote *Pour Your Heart into It,* on how to build a great brand; and business professor Noel Tichy, who was once head of training for GE and who writes frequently on leadership. I mean, it's one thing for David Novak to get up there and tell the people in his company how they all need to think of themselves as teachers, but it's something else when Noel Tichy gets up there and tells them. People love learning from superstars. And because I enjoy learning as much as I enjoy teaching, I love making it happen. It gets us all out of our routine and gives us an outsider's perspective.

More recently, we've had many of our own people develop programs on specific subjects. Sam Su, for instance,
our head of Yum! in China, has developed a program on
how to make good decisions. Graham Allan, the president
of our international division, has developed a program
called Big Leap Forward to develop the potential of general
managers. Taken as a whole, the business leaders, members
of our board, bestselling authors, motivational speakers, and
our own internal experts have helped us develop what we
call Yum! University.

14

The First Year

Coming Together as a Team

We all worked hard to get the company ready to be spun off and to begin establishing the kind of culture we wanted, but obviously, that was just the beginning. With our Founders' Day behind us, we were faced with the enormous task of uniting this huge entity, made up of three independent (sometimes even competitive) restaurant groups and more than 600,000 employees around the world, into one great company.

One of the biggest and, I think, best early decisions we made was to centralize our culture. That was huge because it could have easily gone the other way and we'd be a very different company today. At the time there were people, and plenty of them, telling me it was impossible. The international division in particular was voicing serious resistance. The feeling was that you can't transfer values because values are local and cultures are different. In Asia, for example, people were thought to be too formal and wouldn't like spontaneous recognition. "Giving away a floppy chicken would be considered an insult," someone said.

I hadn't had any international experience at that point

in my career, so I was wrestling with whether to believe what people were telling me. But then Peter Hearl, the executive VP of our international division, finally said to me, "Look, David, I've traveled all over the world, worked in multiple countries, and that's absolute bull. Good values are universal. We need to have one culture for everyone in the company, no matter where they are."

That gave me the courage to do what I already knew in my heart I really wanted to do. We had established our values; now I wanted to make driving our culture around the world my number one priority.

Recognition Works Everywhere

My first international trip as vice chairman was to Singapore, where I got to see firsthand how the values we'd established on paper were being put into practice. Wendy came along, and one afternoon we decided to go to lunch at KFC. There was one in a mall near our hotel, so we went over there, introduced ourselves, had a nice meal, and left.

We were walking away from the restaurant when we heard someone yelling my name, "Mr. Novak! Mr. Novak!" We turned around to see this pregnant woman running after us. When she caught up to us and caught her breath, she introduced herself as Carol Tan, the local area coach. Then she said, "I had to tell you, I recently participated in one of your leadership seminars with my team, and they gave me all this terrible feedback. They told me I didn't listen, that I didn't recognize them enough, that I needed to get them more involved in the success of our restaurant. I was really upset at first, but then I realized what they were saying and that I could do better." Then she pulled out her I Will card. (In our leadership program we give out these wallet-sized cards on which people can write down what they want to work on about themselves. For example, mine says, "I will stay focused on our people.") On hers she had written, "I will be better at . . ." and then listed every suggestion she had gotten from her team. She was so excited about it that after she was finished, I pulled out my own I Will card and read to her what I was working on.

When we finally left the mall, Wendy, who had been mostly quiet during the exchange, looked at me and said, "I guess all this culture stuff you're always talking about really does work!"

Since then, I've had the privilege of hearing story after story proving that it does work, and every one of them is inspiring. Jess Montemyer, who is our successful KFC franchisee in the Philippines, told me that when he got feedback from his team for the first time, it was really bad. They made it really clear he was too harsh on his people. After that, he made a 180 and took appreciating his team members to a whole new level. He organized a retreat for them in the mountains where they could talk about the business and how to make it better. What struck me about his story was the measurable effect that that time spent with his employees had on his bottom line. Up until then, his business had always suffered losses of about 5 to 6 percent due to theft, but after the retreat, that number went down to 1 percent.

I got to witness one of the more moving examples of

our culture at work when Francisco Rivera, who has built a highly successful Pizza Hut business in El Salvador, invited me to his quarterly meeting. Four times a year he invites all the people who have been promoted to a hotel to celebrate their success. He has a ceremony for them where they are recognized in front of their peers, but what really makes it special is the surprise that follows. Once everyone is up onstage, he throws open the doors of the auditorium and in walk the families of the honorees. Kids come running up to greet their fathers or mothers, and it's a really emotional moment. Practically everyone is in tears by the end of ceremony, even me!

Recognition works everywhere—I've seen it with my own eyes—but no matter how many times I say it, there are always doubters. I was recently asked to give a speech on our corporate culture to students of the business school at Peking University in Beijing. I talked about the importance of reward and recognition, and then I had Lily Zhao, who opened our very first store in China twenty years ago in Tiananmen Square and who now runs 150 stores in all, come up onstage to receive my Yum! award.

Most of the students seemed convinced, but one voiced that same concern that I've heard before: Was I forcing American culture on the Chinese when I did this kind of stuff? I told him I had learned over the years that people love to be recognized for the good work they do no matter who they are or where they come from and that I believed the Chinese were no different from anyone else in that way. The crowd erupted in applause.

It occurred to me later that I got the same reaction in Beijing that I had gotten at the University of Missouri when I gave the same speech not long before. I have always firmly believed, and now I have proof, that the desire to be valued is at the root of every culture.

Show Your Face

Thankfully, I wasn't starting from scratch when it came to establishing one culture. As I've already explained, my ideas had already been put into practice and were pretty well entrenched at KFC. I hadn't been head of Pizza Hut for all that long before the spin-off, but it was long enough to have begun to make an impact there, too. Taco Bell was different. I hadn't had much contact with the people there, but I knew enough about it to understand that it was going to be a challenge. There were even some rumblings early on that Taco Bell wanted to spin off on its own.

Taco Bell headquarters is located in Irvine, California, and the culture there at the time was "California corporate," which basically means it was a dress-casual version of the same executive-driven, top-down culture that they had at PepsiCo. People there had already heard about what I'd done at KFC, and the popular opinion seemed to be "That may work in Louisville, but it's not cool enough for us here in California."

Besides the fact that its headquarters was on the West Coast, Taco Bell was also the youngest of our three brands, which may partially explain why it always felt different from the others. It was founded by Glen Bell, a World War II veteran and former hot dog stand owner, in California at a time when most of America had never even heard of a taco. Bell was a savvy businessman from the beginning who started out in the restaurant business selling hot dogs and hamburgers in his hometown of San Bernardino, California (coincidentally, the McDonald brothers opened their first place not far away). But Bell himself loved eating at the local Mexican restaurants, and he particularly loved tacos. The only problem was, they took a really long time to make. He was certain that the rest of America would love the taco, too, if only he could find a quick way to bring it to them.

Sure that he was on to something, Bell decided to test out his theory in a nearby Mexican neighborhood. That way, if it worked, "potential competitors would write it off to the location and assume that the idea wouldn't sell anywhere else," he said.

Bell started off by selling hot dogs and tacos together. In fact, Taco Bell's taco sauce was adapted from his recipe for chili-dog sauce. Only after he perfected his fast-food taco recipe and the item took off did he build several outlets devoted solely to tacos. The first, a simple walk-up taco stand, was completed in 1954. Eight years later he had honed his business model and opened the first stand with the name Taco Bell, in Downey, California. Soon he opened eight more stands in the Los Angeles area, all of which are still there today.

One of Bell's innovations was the idea of saturating a neighborhood. Up until then, the prevailing wisdom was, if your business is doing well, then why would you want to open another one across the street? (Plus, in a franchise system, there are often territory issues, like the one the KFC franchisees were fighting with PepsiCo over when I became president.) But Bell took the opposite approach, building multiple restaurants in a single neighborhood to eliminate the competition. It's a strategy that's widely used today by companies like Starbucks, Barnes & Noble, and many others, and it worked for Bell. From there, business spread like wildfire. Taco Bell became a public company in 1969, and Bell retired as chairman of the board in 1975. Three years later, the company was sold to PepisCo.

To begin to bring Taco Bell into the fold, the first thing I did was simple: I went out west to show them my face. Taco Bell had a fall business conference of all its franchisees in Colorado Springs, and I gave a speech there about why the spin-off was going to be good for all of us, how we were going to be a restaurant-focused company (unlike PepsiCo), and how we were going to leverage our scale.

It was an okay speech, but these were seasoned businesspeople and they'd heard good speeches before. Sometimes the best thing you can do to really get someone's attention, to make them sit up and take notice, is to just be different from the person who came before you. Luckily for me, the former and most famous CEO of Taco Bell, John Martin, was almost the complete opposite of me personality-wise, which made it that much easier.

Don't get me wrong; I admire John a lot. In fact, I think of him as one of the better business minds I've ever known, and he did a lot to build the Taco Bell brand. But he didn't have much love for franchisees, and the feeling was mutual. The franchisees still tell a story about him showing up at one of their meetings on a motorcycle, giving a speech, and then driving off without talking to anyone. That was definitely not my style—neither the motorcycle nor the quick getaway.

The first thing I did to change things up was to take questions after my speech. I knew that a lot of people would be skeptical about the change, so I let them voice their concerns. I answered by telling them that in our organization, one plus one was going to equal three; we were going to be partners who listened to each other, and together we were going to come up with ideas and solutions that were far better than either side could come up with on its own. That seemed to register with a lot of people.

Next, I went to their family picnic after the meeting. Wendy was with me, and the two of us walked around and introduced ourselves, and then we sat down to dinner. That really hit home for people because it was so different from John. Make no mistake, I knew that these were hard-nosed businesspeople and that our future relations were really going to depend on performance—if sales were good, then they would like our new company; if they were bad, then they wouldn't—but I also knew after that that they'd at least give me and my ideas a fair shot.

Crises Breed Trust (If You Do the Right Thing)

I'd gotten off on the right foot with the franchisees, but I didn't completely earn their trust until later, when we encountered our first big crisis. An environmental organization had released a report saying that StarLink, a GMO (genetically modified organism), had been found in Kraft Taco Bell taco shells sold in grocery stores. StarLink had not been approved by the FDA for human consumption, so even though there was no real safety risk, it became a big story all over the country. The late Peter Jennings covered a story on it for the ABC *Evening News.*

In cases like these you have to respond to the public's perception of the problem as much as to the facts of the situation. It didn't matter that if there were GMOs in the taco shells, they weren't likely to hurt anyone. And it didn't matter that GMOs were never found in our restaurant taco shells, just the ones sold in supermarkets by Kraft via a licensing agreement. What mattered was that our customers were scared to eat at Taco Bell because Kraft immediately pulled its taco shells from the supermarket shelves.

The result of that GMO scare was that sales across the country declined 20 to 25 percent. That was a big blow to our Taco Bell franchisees at a time when sales had already gone flat.

The association of Taco Bell franchisees called me up about a month after the StarLink announcement and asked me to come to a summit in Pinehurst, North Carolina, that they had organized because their system was in real trouble. Their sales were down, many of their people were near bankruptcy, and the publicity was killing them. It was a real mess and a potential mutiny in the making.

Of course, none of this was Yum!'s fault. They knew that we were under no obligation to help them out. But if we didn't, many of the franchisees were going to go under.

Within the company, thought was divided about what

we should do. A lot of people felt that the company should not assume the risk of bailing out the franchisees. If stores went under, we could always buy them back at a low price. But we came to have a different view. I told the franchisees that we were going to support them, and we did. The first thing we did was set up a team led by our finance people to work with the banks to restructure their debts. We also sued the supplier who provided the taco shells and then gave every penny of our recovery, which was a lot of money, back to the franchisees. We absorbed all the costs of doing both these things, passing none of them on to the franchisees, and in exchange, all we asked was that if we were going to become their partners in this crisis, then none of them could sue or go public against us, or the deal would be off.

All the franchisees hung in there and remained viable, and sales eventually turned around. In fact, Taco Bell had five straight years of same-store sales growth after that, and is now the second-most-profitable quick-service brand in the United States, behind only McDonald's.

Following the crisis, the Taco Bell franchisees asked me to attend a special meeting. Something incredible happened there. These people, who just a few years earlier had threatened to try to spin off on their own, made a big presentation to thank me for our support. They called what we had done for them "heroic" and gave me this four-foot-high Superman statue with my face on it. I still have it in my office. Afterward, every single one of them lined up to thank me personally, telling me things like "I want you to know, my family wouldn't have its business today if it weren't for you." It was one of the most emotional experiences I've ever had in business. Nothing bonds people better than a big crisis, and relations with the Taco Bell franchisees have been fantastic ever since.

There's Power in One

Having one cohesive culture for all our brands was not just about feel-good working-togetherness. It made good, practical business sense as well.

We set "oneness" as an initial goal for the new company because it seemed obvious to me that the three brands working independently of one another as part of PepsiCo had not been entirely successful. For one thing, the brands competed against one another, so you might find a KFC and a Taco Bell, for example, bidding on the same space in the same neighborhood and driving up the price.

If we could get everyone working together, we would have some serious power to leverage our scale. This is where the goodwill we'd been working so hard to build up with the franchisees of all the brands was going to really help us out. Our first test came when we decided to renegotiate our Pepsi beverage contract. After the spin-off we had an agreement with Pepsi that it would supply all our restaurants for five years, but after the contract ran out, we were free to leave Pepsi if we wanted to. We decided to renegotiate that agreement early on to see what we could get.

Rather than having each brand negotiate its own deal, we wanted one beverage-supply contract for all our restaurants. We brought in our board member, Home

Depot cofounder Ken Langone, to help us out because he had connections at Coke. The possibility that Pepsi could potentially lose the business of all three restaurants—and to Coke no less—put us in the driver's seat.

This was the first time that the franchisees from all three brands came together on anything, and it proved my theory that they could do it. Pepsi was happy because it was assured of being the sole supplier to all our restaurants in the future, and we were happy because we got a phenomenal price and better service—a classic win-win.

Showing Faith Can Be a Powerful Tool (Particularly When You Don't Have a Choice)

That success led to the formation of our purchasing cooperative. Under PepsiCo, the restaurant brands all bought their food products separately. Pizza Hut and Taco Bell purchased through a corporate group set up for that very purpose, while KFC had its own purchasing group made up of KFC franchisees. That group ran totally independently of the company, and the KFC franchisees liked it that way.

There was a great debate about the idea when I first brought it up because there is power in owning the supply chain. The purchasing co-op I'd proposed would be owned jointly by corporate and the franchisees, which meant that we would be ceding some of our power to Taco Bell and Pizza Hut, while KFC would be ceding some of its power to us. There were a lot of reasons why this made people on both sides uncomfortable.

I listened to all the arguments, but, at the end of the day, Andy and I decided to put our faith in the franchisees. We knew we wouldn't lose money because, as I've said before, franchisees are entrepreneurs. They're smart and innovative, and they'll never leave a penny on the table.

It took a full year of negotiations before we got everyone aligned, but we now buy food for all our restaurants through our jointly owned cooperative. Today, the franchisees own 75 percent of the co-op (because they own 75 percent of the restaurants) and we own only 25 percent, so we really have put our faith in them. But it has worked out incredibly well. Collectively, we buy about five billion dollars' worth of goods every year, which makes us the biggest buyer of food products in the world. We're the biggest buyer of lettuce, the biggest buyer of cheese, and so on. That gives us enormous leverage in cutting deals with suppliers. But just as important is the fact that we've established an organization that has a common interest across all our brands. In addition to the purchasing co-op, we were also able to consolidate our real estate planning (so none of the brands would ever bid against one another for real estate again), share services such as accounting so that we could have one accounting department instead of three, and consolidate our national media network buying to get better prices.

Surround Yourself with
Opinionated People

Bob Dylan has a song called "Gotta Serve Somebody," and that's the way it should be. Even head honchos have people whom they are obligated to listen to or even take orders from, who remind them that they aren't infallible. As we've seen recently with some high-profile corporate failures, big problems can pop up when no one is questioning the people at the top. But I'm not just talking about corruption and fraud, I'm also talking about simply making good decisions. Even leaders with the best of intentions can have dumb ideas sometimes, and if you have good people around you, then hopefully they'll stop you before you've done too much damage.

Andy, as I said, assembled an all-star team for our board, and we couldn't have been more blessed. They knew just when to ask questions and when to back off and let us do our thing. I learned how important their contribution was very early in the game, after only our second board meeting, when I came in all pumped up with the idea of building a new corporate headquarters.

The proposal for a new building had come out of the fact that there was so much enthusiasm about the new company, and trust me, I was the one beating the drum the loudest. I wanted to create the look of the leader by having a new campus and a world-class training center. The board didn't say no to the idea, but they did ask a whole lot of questions. They wanted to know not just what it would cost, but what we'd be getting for that money, and they encouraged us to explore all the options.

I went back to the team working on the project and began an entirely new discussion with them. We never did build the thing. At the end of the day we all realized that it wouldn't look very good to spend money building a brand-new headquarters while we were still nearly five billion dollars in debt, not to mention the fact that we already had a headquarters that was at least functional at the time. Thanks to the board, I came to the conclusion that it was one of those "What was I thinking?" moments, and they let me figure it out on my own by asking the right questions.

Celebrate Performance, but Perform Before You Celebrate

That first year I learned another big lesson about keeping our priorities straight. Before our launch, we had asked the new presidents of each division to send in their forecasts for the first year. We were a new company, but the restaurant groups themselves were ongoing operations, so this shouldn't have been such a big deal. Still, somehow, at the end of our first year, we managed to be, collectively, $100 million below our forecast.

This is when I saw how really tough Andy could be. He fired off a scathing memo to the division presidents that I called "the Memo Heard 'Round the World." He really let everyone have it, talking about responsibility, accountability, and how, as a public company that no longer had Mother PepsiCo to back us up, we could not be making these kinds of mistakes. He was right and everyone knew it.

Meanwhile, prior to the forecasting debacle, I had scheduled a big meeting of executives in Keystone, Colorado, where I had invited spouses and kids because I wanted to reinforce our culture and share our vision. I wanted it to be a watershed event that would show just how different and better we would be without PepsiCo. I was trying to shock the system. But as it became more and more clear that we were not going to be able to live up to our first-year projections, Keystone started to look less and less like a good idea—like playing the fiddle while Rome burned.

Ultimately, I decided we couldn't do it, so I canceled the whole thing. Even though I was really fired up about communicating our new direction, it was going to have to wait. Going through with it would have sent the absolute wrong signal. The truth is, we just hadn't earned that sort of celebration yet. And I want to emphasize "yet"!

15

Reward and Recognize, Part 3

Appreciating the Power of People

When we started Yum! I told our people I envisioned a company with the performance-driven culture of GE, the store focus of Wal-Mart, the people focus of Southwest, and the recognition culture of Mary Kay. Blending these elements together would, I believed, give Yum! a unique personality.

While we've made progress on all these fronts, the thing Yum! is probably best known for today is our recognition culture; companies are now visiting us to learn how we use it to drive performance.

We're a company full of awards—whether they're stars, smiley faces, boomerangs, magnets, or crystal trophies. We're overflowing with smiles, applause, cheers, high fives, handshakes, thank-you notes, banners, kudos, and so much more. We do all this because it's far and away the most important way we can express that we are a different kind of company, one that truly appreciates the contributions of its people.

The power of simply acknowledging someone for a job well done is universal. I once heard Colin Powell, when he was giving a speech to my group at PepsiCo, tell a story about a summer job he had as a kid mopping the floors at a bottling plant. He pretty much kept to himself while he was there, but at the end of the summer, a supervisor came up to him and said, "Son, you've done a really good job here." Powell thought his dedication had gone completely unnoticed, so those words had a huge impact. It was a lesson he remembered, and as he rose through the military ranks, he made sure he recognized good work in his subordinates.

When I talked to Bill Miller, our number one Pizza Hut restaurant general manager, he told me that the secret to his success is as simple as the words "thank you." At the end of every shift, he'd make a point of going around to every employee, finding something he'd done well, and thanking him for it. So if there weren't any spots on the silverware one day, he'd go over to the dishwasher and say, "The silverware looks really great today. Thank you!" It's such a simple principle, but it made all the difference to his team members as well as to the success of his restaurant. Thanks to Paul, I now believe "Thank you" is probably the most important thing a leader can say.

Help Your People Feel a Part of Something

Some of the things we do to recognize our people might strike you as too corny to be effective, so if you don't want to take my word for it, or the word of the people at my company, then how about the word of leadership expert

Noel Tichy, a professor at the University of Michigan and the former chief of General Electric's world-famous Crotonville Leadership Center. Here's what he has to say on the subject: "To outsiders, the rituals and symbols of any institution can look silly. But when they are sincere and linked to the values of the organization, they fulfill a deep human need to be connected and to be a part of something and to feel energized as a result."

This is the case whether your organization is made up of financial wizards or factory workers.

Tichy also makes the point that it has to come from the top. If I don't totally embrace the power of recognition myself (and the goofier the better), then ipso facto, it's phony. Recognition doesn't mean just hanging someone's picture on the wall under an Employee of the Month sign. It has to be personal. It has to really mean something to the person receiving it. That's the problem I had back at Pepsi with that self-important-looking plaque. It had no personality, and it had nothing to do with the personality of the person giving it. It was mass-produced, assembly-line recognition.

There are four basic principles behind the kind of reward and recognition we do in our company:

- *Make it fun.* That's why we have parties, a recognition band, and goofy awards like walking teeth and rubber chickens.

- *Be spontaneous.* Catching someone by surprise—when they're least expecting it—adds to the dramatic effect.

- *Make it personal.* This adds the human touch, like giving a little part of yourself.

- *Always be on the lookout for reasons to celebrate the achievements of others.* That's *always*, not just on the second Tuesday of every month. Make it a part of the way you do business every day.

Make It Personal

When I first started talking about the power of recognition, I sometimes felt like a missionary in a foreign country. Now it's almost like preaching to the choir. The proof of the power of recognition is all around me. People from inside and outside of our company now tell me about their own recognition awards and the impact they've made on their own people.

Leaders at all levels of Yum! are required to create their own version of the floppy chicken, the cheese head and the walking teeth. I have found that people now see this as an opportunity, not an obligation. Some of our leaders from other countries make recognition a reflection of their heritage. In Canada, for example, there's the Maple Leaf Award. In Singapore, there's the Tiger Award, because the tiger is an important part of their culture. In Mexico, one of our people gives out an Eagle Warrior Award, using a symbol from Aztec culture.

Personalizing awards is key because it really makes people understand how sincere you are. That's why I write something personal on each one of my awards. Jo Self, our employee program coordinator, recently gave me her recognition award, a silver fortune cookie inside an Asian box. Inside each fortune cookie she places a handwritten "fortune quote" that she has found to describe that person's unique contribution. The one she chose for me was from Marcus Aurelius Antoninus: "Waste no more time talking about great souls and how they should be. Become one yourself."

Of course I loved it—who wouldn't?—because I was being recognized.

Cascade the Message

One of the biggest challenges we face in a company our size is "cascading"—getting our message to reach all levels of the organization. We've done this successfully with our recognition awards, and it's an accomplishment I'm more proud of than anything. Recognition programs can now be seen at every level of our company in every division around the world, and just reading through a list of them shows off the amazing creativity of the people in our organization. Here are just a few examples:

- *The "Show Me the Money" Award.* Since his job is all about watching the dollars and cents, our CFO, Rick Carucci, gives away a piggy bank full of money and a copy of the movie *Jerry Maguire* to those people in his department who have added value to the company through their work.

- **The Pink Bunny Award.** The president of Pizza Hut, Scott Bergren, gives a pink bunny to those people who demonstrate innovation, who have shown they can pull a rabbit out of a hat.

- **The Cover Award.** Qun Wang, our VP of public affairs and government relations in China, puts the honoree's picture on a mock *Time* magazine cover to recognize those who have provided great support for the company's public relations efforts.

- **The Ivey League Award.** The ivy plant is a symbol of knowledge and success, as well as strength and determination. For that reason (and because his last name is Ivey) our chief people officer for KFC, Richard Ivey, gives this award to people who have exhibited these qualities.

- **The Dragon Award.** In China, the dragon is a symbol of strength, superiority, and greatness, so the president of our China division, Sam Su, gives this award to people who provide consistent and significant contributions to the development of our brands in that country.

- **The Grand Scale Award.** Our VP of internal audits, Mary Nixon, gives out a kitchen scale with one of her favorite recipes attached because her job is all about measuring things and because her passion is gourmet cooking. "It's a little about what we do and a little about who I am," she says. That's the best description I've ever heard for how to make an award truly personal. I love it!

- **The Magic 8 Ball Award.** At Pizza Hut, our senior director of research and development, Kathy Nelson, gives a Magic 8 Ball to people who don't take no for an answer and who go above and beyond to make the magic happen.

- **The People Grower Award.** Our senior director of people development at Taco Bell, Mark Wilson, gives mustard seeds and a trowel as a symbol of those people who have been instrumental in helping others grow and develop as individuals.

- **The Footprint Award.** Judy Marschlowitz, a customer-service and recognition coach at Taco Bell, presents a plaster footprint to people who have left a positive impression.

In addition we have the Fasten Your Seat Belt Award, the World Famous Bucket Award, the Camel Award, the Court of the Chancellor Award, the Arrow of Leadership Award, the Yellow Brick Award, the Golden Great Wall Award, the Pressing for Profits Award, the Smart with Heart Award, the Taj Award, the Making Change Award, and on and on and on.

One last important point: Recognition isn't hard to do. You don't need any special equipment or new technologies. It doesn't require a lot of investment. So really, there's no reason not to try it. Give it a shot, and then see how much fun you can have while getting better results from your team at the same time!

16

Steal from the Best

Accelerating My Learning

A ndy Pearson made the announcement in the summer of 1999 that I would become the CEO at the beginning of the following year while he would keep the chairman's title. I thought it was a heck of a way to start off the new millennium. But since I had already been doing a lot of the business of running the company, I also figured the change could end up being largely symbolic unless I did something about it. I had already learned that it was absolutely critical to hit the ground running.

Make an Impact in the First Ninety Days

Before the announcement was made, the CEO of Young & Rubicam, Tom Bell, called me up to tell me about a study he had done on how new CEOs have made their entries into companies. What he told me really got me thinking about how becoming the CEO would be more than a title change for me: "When you become CEO, you'll have people's attention. They'll be watching you to see what you're going to do, so let them know what your agenda is. You have a real chance to make an impact, but you have to do it in the first ninety days. Otherwise they'll think it's going to be business as usual." That's great advice for anyone who gets promoted or starts a new job.

I decided to take this opportunity to define an even clearer vision for how we were going to take our company to new heights. Andy and I had made a lot of progress getting the company off the ground, defining our culture, and consolidating our brands, and we agreed it was time to take things to the next level.

I had already started the learning process by organizing a tour of some of the best companies out there to find out exactly what it was that made them great. I went back to the Partners' Council and asked them to help me study the best practices of the best companies we could find. We would then use those findings to help us strengthen our company. By getting the partners involved, I knew we'd all own whatever conclusions we made. Best-practice visits are done so often in the corporate world as to seem almost meaningless, but for us they were really inspiring. We not only learned from the best, we got to see other leaders in action. When we visited Ken Langone, a director of Home Depot and the investment banker who took the company public, he was out there in the parking lot rounding up shopping carts and returning them to the front of the store, because that's what they want every associate at Home Depot to do, no matter how high up. Then, as we were walking into the store with him, a mentally challenged employee ran up to Ken and asked if he could show him something he'd done that he was really proud of. Ken left us standing there for ten minutes while he went with him to see what he had accomplished. Seemingly small actions like these signal to an entire organization that the way you truly take care of business is by taking care of your people.

Stand on the Shoulders of Giants

The truth of the matter is, there is no reason to try to reinvent the wheel. Most good ideas are already out there, and to learn about them, all you have to do is ask the right people. There's real power in wiping out the "not invented here" syndrome. It multiplies your idea capacity, and there's no need to feel bad about taking someone else's idea and running with it. Believe me, when we do things well in our company, there's a whole line of people ready to steal from us, too. As Micky Pant, our head of international marketing, puts it (paraphrasing Sir Isaac Newton): "This isn't stealing; it's standing on the shoulders of giants."

Here are just a few of the things we learned from some of the top companies we visited in 1999, when they were at the top of their game (some of them still are):

Wal-Mart: "The More You Know, the More You Care"

What surprised me right away was the whole fleet of Wal-Mart planes I saw when we landed at the Bentonville, Arkansas, airport. Now, this is probably the most cost-conscious company in the world, but it was investing in what seemed like an air force of company planes so executives could get out into the field, visit stores, stay in touch with their people at the store level, and see firsthand how programs were being executed.

A junior person from technical services picked me up at the airport, and as we got to talking, I realized that he knew everything about the company, not just his little corner of it. He talked about the stock price, the culture, the challenges. You would have thought I was talking to the president of the company. It was the same way with everyone I spoke to there. Wal-Mart's leaders had obviously made a point of educating and informing everyone at all levels about all aspects of the company, and that shows a real respect for their people.

When we arrived at Wal-Mart headquarters, I noticed a sign in the lobby that said, TODAY'S STOCK PRICE IS X, TOMORROW'S IS UP TO YOU. That impressed me so much, we now have the same sign in our lobby.

What had the biggest impact on me were the systems they had in place for keeping communication flowing, which make a big company feel like a small one. Sam Walton really believed that "the more you know, the more you care," so twenty years ago he created a satellite system. It was his version of the Internet and connected all the stores through their own TV network. If, for example, there was a great display of bicycles in Cedar Falls, Iowa, he could show it off to the people in all his stores through this network and say, "Let's see your version of this display by Monday of next week." Then he'd check in with everyone the following week. Even though he couldn't travel to all the stores all the time, this system gave him a way to stay in touch with his people as his business grew. People felt like they knew

Sam even though they never met him. These kinds of high-touch things really make a difference in a big organization.

Home Depot: "I'm an Owner"

I wanted to visit Home Depot after I read *Built from Scratch* by the cofounders of the company, Bernie Marcus and Arthur Blank. In it, they talk about their passion for customer service. Bernie Marcus, in particular, was known for being the ultimate customer guy. You could see the effects of that all around you in their stores. When we got there, one of the first things we noticed was that the front-line people were stock owners; we knew that because on their aprons they had printed I'M AN OWNER, ASK ME.

Because of that attitude, Home Depot managed to cultivate incredible customer loyalty. The company even published a book of stories from their customers about Home Depot employees who had gone above and beyond the call of duty with great customer service. We started collecting and telling our own customer stories after I heard that. Now we often start out our meetings by sharing inspiring examples of outstanding customer service we hear about or see around the world.

Southwest Airlines: "Put Your People First—and Everything Else a Distant Second"

As I mentioned before, when I first met with Andy Pearson to talk about our priorities for the new company, I had him read *Nuts,* the story of Southwest Airlines, as an example of the kind of company I wanted to build. It is a company that's totally focused on developing its people, so of course it was a place I wanted to see firsthand. As a symbol of that, its whole building is decorated with pictures of the history and events of Southwest and the people who work there. The company also does lots of recognition and believes in having fun. Sometimes the best thing you can get from others is validation of what you're already doing yourself, and that's what I got from Southwest.

Southwest Airlines has been such a people-first model for me for so long that it was inspiring just to be physically in a place I already knew so much about. Yet I didn't fully understand just how far they are willing to go to get the "right people in the right seats" until well after our best-practices tour—when someone I know applied for an entry-level position with the company.

After a one-hour interview over the phone with human resources, Southwest got back to her and told her she had made the first cut of a rigorous interview process. After that she was told she was one of eight candidates they wanted to meet in person. At this point she felt like she had already won a small victory, but she was also told that Southwest Airlines likes to promote from within and that half the candidates were already working there, so there was no need to pop the champagne yet.

At the Southwest office, she was interviewed by not just one but several people from the team—and *at the same time as all the other candidates.* They wanted to see how the candidates interacted with one another. Then, after about an hour, the same group of people interviewed her by herself.

You can imagine how she felt when she got the call saying she had the job. Also, she now knew several of the team members and they knew her, so by the time she actually started, she felt as if she had already been working there.

Sometimes you think you're doing a pretty good job at something until you learn about someone who is doing it so right, it completely redefines the process. We're now big believers in group interviewing.

Target: "Differentiate Yourself"

We went to Target to learn about brand building. Target was always a solid but typical retail company competing with Wal-Mart—until it was able to break away through branding. Today its bull's-eye logo is almost more recognizable in the United States than the Nike swish.

Its tagline is "Expect more, pay less," and it promotes that concept in everything it does. Target has differentiated its brand, making it more hip and cool ("Tar-jay"), through its innovative ad campaigns and by doing tie-ins with such famous designers as Isaac Mizrahi and architect Michael Graves. The image it's created for itself has made Wal-Mart look staid by comparison (which is one of the reasons why Wal-Mart has struggled in the years since we visited). Target's CEO, Bob Ulrich, who just retired from our board after nearly ten years, says that every year someone comes to him and suggests that they could save money if they just narrowed the aisles a few inches. "But that doesn't differentiate our brand in the way we want," he always says. Instead, they keep them wider than everybody else's. My key takeaway: Know what your brand stands for, and exaggerate it in everything you do.

UPS: "Make What Matters Most a Science"

UPS excels by making its drivers its main focus, the center of its universe. They've studied everything there is to know about the driver—the driver mind-set, how they get into their trucks, what their seats are like, what slows them down, what makes things easier for them—resulting in ergonomically designed seats and a shorter step-up into the trucks.

UPS has built a science around what matters most to its business, which is process and discipline around driver efficiency. We immediately put what we learned from UPS to use by reevaluating the science around our Pizza Hut delivery drivers.

General Electric

All the people we met at GE had a tremendous dedication to continuously topping themselves. Jack Welch called it "the relentless drumbeat for performance," and he felt strongly that if you want people to focus on quality, then you need to measure and reward the behaviors that create it. To that end, GE adopted the Six Sigma system, a highly disciplined way of measuring how good its people and procedures are at delivering quality products and services to their customers. I was particularly impressed by how focused the GE folks were at sharing best practices that occurred "inside" the company. Being as big as it is can either make you slow and bureaucratic or help you leverage your scale and know-how for a major competitive advantage. I walked away realizing that our size was a great opportunity. We had more than thirty thousand restaurants, which were like thirty thousand laboratories. My job was to find out what was working best and spread it like wildfire.

The Oracle of Omaha

My own best-practices tour included not just legendary companies, but legendary people as well. When it came to dealing with Wall Street, I was new to the game, and Warren Buffett was obviously the master. I had always dreamed of meeting him. Buffett was on the board of Coke, so I called up Coke's CEO, Doug Ivester, whom I knew from our best-practices visits, to see if he could set something up for me. Ivester told me Buffett agreed on one condition: "I'm not going to talk about your stock." That was fine with me.

I first met Warren at his Berkshire Hathaway offices in Omaha, Nebraska. He told me he liked KFC, so we went there for lunch. One of the first things I asked him was "How should I deal with Wall Street?"

In typical Buffett style, he gave an answer that was so simple it was brilliant. He said: "Don't romance Wall Street. You don't want investors who are only concerned about the quarter, or who are working on their exit strategy from day one. You want shareholders to own you forever. If we have no trading at all, I consider that a tremendous accomplishment."

He went on to explain that getting the right shareholders takes time, and it happens by communicating well, by being up-front about your company—its successes *and* its failures—and what your strategies are to keep it on track. "Talk to your owners," he said. "Tell them there are two kinds of companies. The first is a company where you only need to be right once. That's what it was like to buy a network TV affiliate fifty years ago. The second kind of company is the kind that's in the retail business, where you have to be smart not once but every day. You're in a retail business, and in a competitive category at that, so you're going to have your ups and downs. You have to tell people that but also tell them that you're going to win over time."

Buffett's Wall Street philosophy is to focus on what's right for the long haul and the stock will take care of itself. "If you're honest and do what you say you're going to do on a consistent basis over time, then people will come to trust the company," he said. Finally, he added one caution: "Make sure your ego lies in the performance of the company, not in the performance of the stock."

I got so much out of talking to Warren, I make it a point to go see him every year, and he's generous enough to let me buy him lunch at KFC. In fact, I now take a couple of my high performers along as a reward for a job well done. As most people who know him will tell you, above all else he's just a really nice, down-to-earth guy. One year I brought two Australians from our international team, Graham Allan and Peter Hearl, to meet him, and when we walked in, the first thing we saw was an Australian flag Warren had hung in his office to welcome them. Warren also likes to have fun. Each year we take a picture with the KFC restaurant teams to commemorate our visit, and in every picture you can see him passing one of our people his wallet full of cash.

Warren told me he believes in creating an environment that supports and inspires his people. For many years he would recognize his key executives at his annual stockholders meetings, and his late wife would sing to them "Have I Told You Lately That I Love You?" That's what making people feel appreciated is all about.

Practice Pattern Thinking

One of the qualities I look for when I hire people is pattern thinking, an ability to make connections, pick up on trends, and apply what's going on in the world to your own business. After that best-practices tour, the Partners' Council and I met back at a site in the Adirondacks to do just that—share what we had learned and apply it to our company.

Board member John Weinberg, the chairman of Goldman Sachs, once told me that the truly great companies had 10 percent earnings-per-share growth year after year after year. That was the ambitious goal we decided to set for ourselves. I was inspired by Buffett's long-haul philosophy, so our main task was to discover not what would make us successful this year or the next but what would make us successful for years to come.

All the companies we visited had achieved the kind of greatness we were striving for. When the Partners' Council broke it all down, we realized that we all pretty much admired the same things about those companies. We took everything we learned and came up with five basic things great companies have. I called them "Dynasty Drivers" because the best companies are really like dynasties—they remain strong and viable over a long period. These were the traits that, when we figured out how to put them into practice in our own company, would take us to our overarching goal of building the Yum! Dynasty.

Our Dynasty Drivers have evolved some since then, but they are still basically the same principles that we came up with in the Adirondacks that day:

1. *A culture where everyone makes a difference.* Southwest Airlines epitomized this idea for us. Whether you're a customer service agent or a VP, your contribution matters.

2. *Customer and sales mania.* Home Depot was the standout in this area and made us realize how far we had to go. The best companies are focused on making the customer happy and driving sales. By the way, I think it's fair to say most people think Lowe's is now giving Home Depot a run for its money, which is a reminder that even the leader has to constantly stay on top of its game.

3. *Competitive differentiation.* Target proved how much dedication to this principle can change your business. No matter what a great company decides it stands for, it reinforces that ideal in everything it does and at all levels, whether it's the way it trains its people or presents its brands to the public.

4. *Continuity in people and process.* At every company we visited, the senior management had been with the organization for five to ten years. It's hard to build a winning team if the players change every season, so the best companies value their people and realize that if you help them to continually succeed and improve, then the company benefits. You also have to have processes in place that everyone knows and understands (and that don't change every other week) to help your people achieve their goals. Wal-Mart's communication system and UPS's driver studies were primary examples of this.

5. *Commitment to consistently beating the previous year's results.* The leaders at GE really knew how to effec-

tively raise the bar, and the company had set continual improvement as one of its primary goals. If you want to become a dynasty, you need to always be focused on getting better and beating last year's performance in everything you do. You want to eliminate peaks and valleys, what we call "boom, splat," and go for a good, steady incline.

The Wizard of Westwood

Building a dynasty takes leadership, so I desperately wanted to meet John Wooden, whose ten straight NCAA basketball championships (with at least a 25 percent turnover in "personnel" each year) is the greatest dynasty in sports history. No one else has even come close. Fortunately, one of our franchisees and now a good friend, Eddie Sheldrake, had played basketball for John Wooden at UCLA and helped me arrange a meeting.

I met Mr. Wooden at his home. Here was this titan of sports who could have lived any way he wanted, yet as you might expect, his home was a modest two-bedroom condo with the major "artwork" being pictures of his family, his friends, and his players up on the walls.

The morning I spent with John Wooden were among the most fascinating in my life. He seemed to effortlessly exude wisdom in everything he said. I asked him who had had the greatest impact on his life, and he said his dad, his wife, various coaches, but also Abraham Lincoln. He felt the Gettysburg Address was one of the greatest documents ever written, mainly because Lincoln had said so much with so few words, as opposed to others, "who can talk a lot and not say anything." He was also a big fan of Mother Teresa and her quote "A life not lived for others is not a life."

Coach Wooden told me that his father would always give him advice in "sets of three," like (1) Don't whine; (2) Don't complain; and (3) Don't make excuses, and he himself used this teaching method throughout his life. He said to me, "In my early years I had a lot of rules and a few suggestions. In my latter years I had a few rules and a lot of suggestions. But the three rules I always stuck with were (1) Be on time; (2) No profanity; and (3) Never criticize a teammate."

Coach Wooden spoke in aphorisms ("If you keep too busy learning the tricks of the trade, you may never learn the trade"), while, at the same time, he remained profoundly humble. Of course he considered himself much more of a teacher than a basketball coach. He told me that every year he started off his first practice by teaching the players to put on their shoes and socks correctly so they wouldn't get blisters. He took nothing for granted. But I think the single greatest thing I learned from him that day is this: Your capacity to teach is only as great as your capacity to learn. He was a constant learner. "It's what you learn after you know it all that counts," he said. His curiosity and his passion for knowledge seemed infinite.

My favorite takeaway from that day came after I asked him how he stayed on top of his game after winning a championship. "At the end of every season," Coach Wooden said, "I would take some topic about the game and research it. I might take rebounding, or I might take zone defense, or I might take attacking zones, or I might take the fast break, or I might take a good jump shot. And I would read all of the books written by coaches who I thought excelled in these particular areas. And I would take notes. And then eventually I would make one composite notebook from all these, and then I would study it. For instance, when Lew Alcindor [later Kareem Abdul-Jabbar] first came to play with us, I had never had anyone even approaching his size, and so I contacted Wilt Chamberlain and other coaches who had coached extra-tall players, and talked to them personally to get all the information I could in regard to working with an exceptionally tall and talented player."

Can you imagine deciding to make yourself the world's foremost expert on coaching "extra-tall players"? That was John Wooden. I always show a video of my interview with "Professor Wooden" during my leadership seminars, and what impresses our leaders is how he tried to learn something new every year even though he won ten straight championships. They always conclude "If he can do that, why can't we?"

Take Stock Every Day

Meeting with Coach Wooden, the most humble leader I've ever met, made me think about my ego, about, as the wise John Weinberg once put it, the difference between "growing and swelling."

I must admit, it can be hard to keep your ego in check when you have the top job, and for CEOs it can be an occupational hazard. I know I struggle with it from time to time—at least Wendy tells me so! It's very difficult to work your way to the very top rung without having a pretty high opinion of yourself. I asked Coach Wooden about this, and he said, "Most leaders have enough ego as it is, so you don't need anyone around to inflate it any further. Have strong, opinionated people working for you."

Not too long ago, I asked our board member Bob Ulrich, chairman and CEO of Target, to speak to our marketing people at a global conference. I told him Howard Schultz, founder of Starbucks, had spoken the year before, and I wanted another big name. Bob said that his chief marketing officer, Michael Francis, would give a much better presentation on marketing than he ever could. I told him I wanted a CEO, and he essentially told me to stuff my ego in a drawer and call Francis.

I was a bit insulted, but as it turned out, Bob was right. Francis gave one of the best presentations on brand building I have ever heard, giving example after example of how Target differentiates its brand in everything it does and how it challenges everyone in its stores to be a brand builder.

From our best-practices tour, from meeting with Warren Buffett and Coach Wooden, and from presenting my leadership program so many times, I have finally figured out what I want to be when I grow up. I want to be a teacher. I think the act of teaching is the most gratifying and rewarding of all human endeavors. It's what drives me. When I said at the beginning of this book that my sole purpose in writing it is to teach—to share what I have learned with others—that was totally sincere, but as I work my way toward the end, it occurs to me that it's even more true than I had realized.

Stealing Coach Wooden's sets of three, I have come up with a formula for success no matter what kind of business you happen to be in: (1) Make sure you have the right people around you; (2) Have fun and drive results by recognizing the achievements of others; and (3) Be a passionate learner, and pass on what you know to others. Not only will this make you a success in business, it will make you a success in life.

Share Your Vision

The idea of building a dynasty had me really pumped up, and I couldn't wait to rally the troops behind the notion the same way I'd done for our culture. Forget about the first ninety days, I wanted to make an impression on my very first day as CEO, and I thought those Dynasty Drivers would be a great way to share my new vision with the company.

On New Year's Day of 2000, my first official day as CEO, copies of my handwritten note, with the Dynasty Drivers attached, arrived at the homes of around thirty thousand employees. I wanted to send the message to people at their homes because I wanted to shock their systems. How often do people get a note from the CEO delivered to their homes on a holiday? My hope was that it would spur conversation, that around the dinner table that night people would be talking with their families about making a great company.

And it worked. When people came back to work after the holiday, they were talking about it around the water cooler. Of course, we still had to walk the talk.

17

Be Careful What You Wish For

Managing Adversity

Despite my grand vision for the company, during my first year as CEO, Yum!'s performance was terrible. Our stock plummeted; each U.S. brand, KFC, Taco Bell, and Pizza Hut, showed sales losses, and that was coming off two straight years of doing very well. It had to be Murphy's Law. I finally get a chance to be the one officially in charge, and that's the year we tank.

A Big Crisis Puts You to the Test

If history is a great teacher, maybe from now on I should skip the Super Bowl. My intention was to start my first year off with a bang, but on Super Bowl Sunday, just a couple of weeks after I officially became CEO, I got the call that AmeriServe, the distribution company responsible for transporting *all* our food in the United States from our suppliers to our stores, was in dire financial straits. This was more than just run-of-the-mill bad news. If Ameri-Serve collapsed, our restaurants could go dark and the whole company would be in danger of going under. It's hard to have a restaurant with no food. Forget about the dynasty. We were in survival mode.

We had been riding pretty high up until the Ameri-Serve fiasco. In March of the previous year our stock had hit an all-time high of thirty-six dollars per share. Things were going so well, in fact, that I cockily said in a phone interview with the press that we should have called our company "Yum Dot-Com" because our stock price had skyrocketed as quickly as the dot-coms'. Those were words I would live to regret. Soon afterward, the NASDAQ plummeted five hundred points in two days and the tech bubble burst. Less than a year later, our stock plummeted as well. The primary reason for the fall was the public announcement by AmeriServe that it was declaring bankruptcy. Our stock went as low as thirteen dollars a share, twenty-three dollars lower than it had been just nine months before, proof that you should never take a premature victory lap.

AmeriServe was a hassle that we inherited from PepsiCo. Food distribution had been done by an in-house organization under PepsiCo called PFS. Just before the spin-off, PepsiCo pulled the rug out from under us by selling off that piece of the business to a private company for a tremendous sum of money. We were no longer in control of our food supply. The new company was called AmeriServe, and in order to pay PepsiCo, it started off with a huge amount of debt. But based on the agreement PepsiCo had made, we were stuck with it after the spin-off, whether we liked it or not.

About a year into our new company, we started to get word that AmeriServe was slow in paying its suppliers.

Then we began to hear rumors of nonpayment and that some suppliers were threatening to withhold product unless they got paid in advance. The problem was that because of our contract, all we could do was keep an eye on the situation, hope for the best, and plan for the worst.

You may recall that my worst day at Pepsi was on Super Bowl Sunday when the FCC forced me to cancel our free-two-liter-bottle promotion. Now, on this Super Bowl Sunday, I sent a crack team up to New York to meet with the CEO of AmeriServe to find out just how bad things really were. By the end of that meeting, they were asking us for a big loan to stay afloat. That's when we knew that they were going under, it was just a matter of when.

AmeriServe had been trying to keep the details of the trouble they were in a secret so that their suppliers, who would be on the hook for any defaults in payment if bankruptcy was declared, would continue to do business with them. They even kept it from us. It was just four days later that it filed for bankruptcy in the Delaware courts (because of Delaware's favorable bankruptcy laws), and we didn't hear about it until after the fact. Earlier that same day they had assured us that they were *not* going to declare bankruptcy at all. Four hours later, by hand-scribbled fax, they filed one of the biggest bankruptcies in Delaware history.

When It Hits the Fan . . . Rely on Your Experts

Our mission, at that point, was to keep supplies flowing so that our restaurants never had to shut down. I got on the phone with our major suppliers to assure them that we'd stand with them on this if they'd just keep working with us. Thanks to that and the debtor-in-possession financing granted AmeriServe by the Delaware court, the trucks kept running and we stayed in business.

That bought us some time, but our only viable option was to find someone who would buy AmeriServe out of bankruptcy—not an easy task. We had to make a credible sales presentation to entice a buyer, and in order to do that, we had to band together as a company once again. We got the whole system—the franchisees from all of our brands— to sign on to a single distribution contract even though many of them were free to go off on their own and try to save themselves. We interviewed a lot of potential distributors, and many of them said they didn't want to touch this mess. Once again our efforts at relationship building with our franchisees paid off, and we worked hand in hand to solve the problem. Finally, with the assurance that they'd have the business of one united system with eighteen thousand stores nationwide, we were able to strike a deal with the McLane Company, which successfully handles all our distribution to this day, and a huge crisis was averted.

This whole process took a year and a half. I could have easily gotten bogged down in the endless details of it all, but thankfully, I had a top crisis-management team led by our chief legal counsel, Chris Campbell, who did a lot of the tough sledding.

The ability to delegate is nice in theory, but this really put me to the test. Could I really let someone else handle something this big? Of course I was involved along the way and I was there when the big decisions needed to be made, but I had to trust my team to handle the day-to-day management of the problem because I still had a company to run. If I hadn't done that, I wouldn't have gotten much else done for over a year and I probably would have lost sight of our long-term goal, which was to build a consistently high-performing company. That would have been a disaster in itself. Instead, I chose the best people we had to deal with the problem, and then I let them do their job. My key takeaway: You have to rely on your experts.

Stay Cool and Keep the Faith

I would have preferred it if my first year as CEO had been crisis-free, but the truth is, you can learn more from the bad times than you can from the good. Some of my most valuable lessons over the years have come during our darkest moments.

I first learned about crisis management from Craig Weatherup. In 1993 someone placed syringes in Pepsi cans. It was national news. Craig immediately got on top of the situation and handled everything in a calm manner that only earned the Pepsi brand more loyalty. I'll never forget walking into his office just before he was getting ready to go on national TV. I said, "Craig, what do you do before you go on the Larry King show to talk about something like this?"

He just looked at me like he didn't have a care in the world and said, "I read my mail."

He was at ease because he had total command of his business and complete confidence in the Pepsi bottling process. His demeanor when he appeared on television

talk shows and in the TV commercials Pepsi aired to explain what was going on put the consumer at ease as
well.

Unfortunately, at Yum! we've had food-safety issues of
our own over the years—not many, thankfully, but every
one of them has taken a lot of fun out of the business. In
order to handle them the right way, I take a page from
Craig's book and keep a cool head. When a crisis arises we
go through five basic steps:

- Don't panic.
- Get the facts.
- Make good decisions based on those facts.
- Continually get the word out about how you're
  handling the situation.
- Lay out what you're doing to make sure it doesn't
  happen again.

All the while I challenge our team to be "bullet-proof"
and "weasel-proof" in all communications. Bullet-proof in
the sense that facts are unassailable and weasel-proof in the
sense that people can't say, "Yeah, but you're weaseling out
of the issue by leaving out this fact or that fact." This forces
the team to look at all the "F's" (remember the exercise on
page 171) and all sides of the issue. By the way, this works
with all kinds of difficult issues that require rock solid credibility, like making product claims or convincing franchisees
to make major investments.

And through all of it, you have to stay positive and have
faith in the abilities of your people to work it through. This
is when the power of your culture takes over. We don't get

involved in the blame game. We use positive energy to get the right endgame.

It's times like these when it's critical to have good people on your team to give you the right perspective, and that's what Sam Su did for us in 2004 when we found Sudan Red, a potentially carcinogenic dye, in one of the ingredients we use to prepare New Orleans Chicken in China. The dye had turned up in only very small amounts and wasn't a realistic health threat. Besides, the blame really belonged to our supplier in China, who had provided us with the seasoning mix and assured us it was safe. But none of that mattered. Sam told us that if we were going to have any chance of earning back the trust of both the government and the public, first we would have to apologize publicly.

I didn't like the idea initially, but I knew Sam was right. So apologize is what we did. Then, because you can't eat an apology, we worked with the government to set up a state-of-the-art comprehensive food-safety system, including a product-testing center in China to ensure that it would never happen again.

In a company as big as ours, the unfortunate truth is that we can't avoid situations like this altogether. Obviously, we take food safety very seriously (we wouldn't be in business for very long if we didn't), and we are constantly working to find better processes to ensure safety, but the kinds of stories that make the news are often news to us as well.

I'd like to be able to say that we'll never have a problem like Sudan Red again, but that would be disingenuous. What I can say is that we make a point of learning from every crisis, even the ones that begin with some supplier in China that we don't control. The facility we have

in China for testing food safety is the best we have anywhere, and we send our people there from all over the
world to learn their protocol. If crises can't always be
averted, usually something positive can come from them.

Perception Is Reality

In November 2006, the day before our annual meeting in
New York with Wall Street analysts, we had another big
crisis. People had gotten sick with *E. coli* poisoning in four
states in the Northeast (including New York), and the local
health departments had tracked the source of those illnesses to Taco Bell.

When something like that happens, it's obviously not
only a terrible thing for the people who get sick, but it's
frightening for the public as a whole. Even though the problem was isolated to produce supplied to the Northeast, Taco
Bells all over the country felt the sting of public concern, and
sales declined dramatically. Crises happen, but when public
health is involved, there's no room for messing around.
There's no choice but to do the right thing right away.

The first thing we did when we heard the news (after
not panicking, of course) was work with the government
to find the source of the illnesses. Tracing an illness is a
tricky and cumbersome scientific process. Obviously, it's
difficult to rush it. The pace can be frustrating, like watching paint dry.

The timing of this crisis was unfortunate for us because before we had time to get all the facts, we had to
give our presentation to investors. That morning the news

was in both the *New York Times* and the *Wall Street Journal,* which, of course, all the analysts read. There was no way to hide it, but that wouldn't have been our style anyway. Instead of avoiding the subject and waiting for someone to ask us the inevitable question about it, we decided to start off the meeting with the news, to put it right out there on the table. Tim Jerzyk, our head of investor relations, opened by telling them everything we knew about the crisis and that we thought the press was being very fair and had done a good job reporting it. That got their attention; how many companies praise the press in times like this?

We came off like we had nothing to hide because we hid nothing. (I wish a few politicians would learn to do this.) Amazingly, our stock actually went up that day, which shows the faith the financial community had in our ability to handle the situation. When it came to the question-and-answer part of the program, we didn't hear one question about it.

Transparency is terribly important in a situation like this, as is a quick reaction time, because news today is not only immediate, it travels globally on the Internet. In our YouTube culture, dramatic videos take on a life of their own, beyond anyone's control. That's what occurred in a high-profile incident in New York City when rats were caught on camera in one of our franchise stores. What happened was the franchisee had already hired a pest-control firm to look into this potential problem. After cutting a six-by-one-foot hole in the basement floor (big enough for a German shepherd to crawl through!), the pest-control company left the site around midnight to finish up the next day. At 3:30 A.M., while the store was closed, a passerby noticed that rats had entered through the gaping hole. The news media were called and a video was taken of the rats running around. Of course, there shouldn't have been any rats in the restaurant, period. But in urban areas, some say, rats outnumber people. It's just a fact of life. And today anyone with a cell phone camera is an instant reporter. The video of these rats bounced around the globe (it was the fifth-most-watched video on YouTube at the time). The news reached me at a business conference in Australia within hours of the rats being captured on film, and it's all anyone wanted to talk about. Jay Leno and David Letterman made dirty-rat jokes for well over a week. Not a very proud moment for anyone in our company, including me.

It's always a challenge to not only do the right thing but to be sure you keep the public informed. If any good has come out of the *E. coli* crisis, it's that we realized that our country needs even better health and safety standards for produce, and we're now working with our suppliers and the FDA to accomplish this. As for those famous (and now very dead) rats, we've shut the restaurant for good and we're working with the New York City Health Department and others to deal with pest control every day.

18

Customer Mania

Going Bonkers

My first year as CEO had been a challenging one for sure, but we still managed to keep the company growing and morale high, thanks in large part to our international business, which really began to take off. In 2000, we opened a record 950 new restaurants outside the U.S. market.

With a great team keeping an eye on our AmeriServe troubles, I was able to keep looking forward. One of the things I've learned to do as a leader to continually move us in the right direction is take a page from John Wooden's playbook. Each year I pick one big thing to focus on that I think will make us a better company.

By this point, we had pretty well established a culture and framework for the company. Recognition programs had been started across the globe, more and more people had gotten a chance to take my leadership seminar, and our values were spreading. But when I stepped back and looked around at what I thought we needed to improve, the answer seemed to stick out like a sore thumb.

Even though our passion statement was "to put a yum on customers' faces all around the world" and our number-one How We Work Together tenet was customer focus, we just hadn't lived up to those ideals. At the time, every one of our brands ranked lower than our competitors on customer satisfaction in the United States, and lower than McDonald's internationally. Even though people liked our food and sales were up across the brands, when it came to making our customers happy, we were being beaten out by McDonald's, Del Taco, Domino's, and others.

I usually start thinking in September or October about what aspect of the business I want to concentrate on improving during the following year. In the fall of 2000, when I had this very issue on my mind, I happened to turn on the television and see Jack Welch being interviewed on *60 Minutes*. He was talking about quality. "You know," he said, "if you believe in quality, you can't just tell everybody, 'We believe in quality.' You've got to go bonkers on quality. You've got to measure quality. You've got to pay bonuses based on quality. You've got to let everyone in the organization know that they are being judged on quality."

I loved what he was saying, and the first thing I thought was "What do we need to go bonkers on in our organization?" The answer was clear: We needed to do more than just pay lip service to the idea of customer service. In fact, we needed to go bonkers on it. That's when I came up with the concept of customer mania, not customer satisfaction or customer focus but customer mania. We were going to be maniacs on behalf of our customers.

Being a customer maniac is a Yum! expression we use over and over. We aspire to not simply satisfy the customers, which is somewhat passive, but to actively try to make them feel welcomed and happy to be eating in one of our restaurants—to put a yum on their faces. Happy customers are repeat customers, are more frequent customers, and can be your most powerful form of advertising, which is word of mouth.

Pay Attention to the Power of Language

I love Jack Welch's choice of the word *bonkers*. It's a real break-through-the-clutter word, a word that seems like it was meant to create havoc.

I have a tremendous appreciation for the power of even a single word to create impact, which of course is what I was trying to do with "customer mania." Some people in our company initially thought the word *mania* was too negative. After all, being a "maniac" in front of your customers sounds like it might not be such a good thing. But that was okay, because the word shocked people's systems a little bit and got them thinking about the idea of doing more for the customer. Since much of execution depends on first getting people to pay attention to what really matters, *how* you say something may be just as important as what you are saying.

One of the best examples I've ever heard to illustrate this was when Fairfax Cone of Foote Cone & Belding said that Raid set itself apart from countless other insecticides by adding one redundant word to create one of the most memorable taglines in advertising history: "Raid kills bugs dead!"

If you want to break through the clutter and get people's attention, both in and out of the company, it's worth taking the time to choose the words that will create the greatest impact.

Create a Sense of Urgency

To put it another way, play like you're ten points behind in the final quarter. I've also heard this defined as "operational cadence"—creating a *rat-a-tat-tat* rhythm of doing business that drives the relentless pursuit of results.

Whatever I learned about creating a sense of urgency started when I worked for Howard Davis at Tracy Locke. He really knew how to push people—everything had to be done yesterday—and I was one of the people who got pushed. Howard was a master of intimidation. Everyone knew that if you didn't give him what he wanted, he was going to find another way to get it, and if you weren't part of the solution, then you were part of the problem. The clients loved Howard because they knew he'd kill for them (and none of us wanted to be the one he killed). It wasn't always comfortable, but it taught me the value of constantly putting pressure on myself and the people who work for me. In corporate America, pressure is a way of life, so rather than resist it or merely accept it, you have to learn to use it as a personal motivator.

Creating a sense of urgency around change initiatives is especially hard to do. Human nature seems to be hardwired to abhor change, and people will do everything in their power to resist it. I once heard this explained another way by a consultant at Pepsi. His philosophy was that in order to drive change, you need to create what he called "the burning platform." His burning-platform image was an oil rig in the North Sea that has caught fire and the only way to save yourself is to jump into the frigid water and swim to the lifeboat. You know the jump might kill you, but you jump anyway, not because you think it might be a good idea but because you have no choice. That's creating a sense of urgency.

To begin creating a sense of urgency around customer mania, I went back to my Partners' Council. In their case it was easy; all I had to do was show them the data on our dismal customer-satisfaction ratings. Nobody wants to be in last place. Everyone agreed that we had a major, company-wide problem and that we needed to find a way to start turning things around real quick. I also told the board we would never stop driving and measuring customer mania, and if I did, they should fire me. You can rest assured that created a sense of urgency for me personally that has helped me to keep customer mania at the top of my agenda.

Make It Real

As I said earlier, I believe that when the student is willing, the teacher appears. Around this time, I got a call from Ken

Blanchard, who is a consultant on motivating people and the author of numerous books, including *The One Minute Manager.* He said he wanted to come see me, and we met for breakfast. When I told Ken about our focus on customer mania, he got very excited. One of the things he said to me was that the most important thing we could do to encourage customer mania in our restaurants was to elevate our front-line jobs and do whatever we could to make our people feel important. If they felt good about what they were doing, then that would rub off on our customers.

Later I had Ken come speak to members of my team, and out of that grew our customer-mania training program, which we present quarterly to our restaurant teams each year. (Ken even wrote a book about his views on our company a couple of years later called—what else?—*Customer Mania: It's Never Too Late to Build a Customer-Focused Company.*) The program teaches the basics of good customer relations: how to listen to customers, how to be empathetic, how to exceed customer expectations (within reason), and how to recover when you make a mistake. We've also found ways to empower our people around what's important. For instance, in dealing with unhappy or dissatisfied customers, we give our team members discretion up to a certain dollar amount in substitutions to "make it right" with the customer. This cuts down on people saying, "Let me speak to the manager," gives our employees the satisfaction of solving problems themselves, and helps them buy into our customer-mania philosophy.

I once had a reporter in Germany say to me during an

interview, "Your jobs are so bad I don't know why anyone would want to work for you." She was talking about
our in-store jobs—the counter people, the cooks, the
people who take your order at the drive-thru. I know
these aren't the highest-paid positions out there, but I
had to disagree with her. Thanks to our customer training, every one of our employees learns basic life skills that
they can use no matter what they end up doing. We've
had people go on to become doctors, lawyers, veterinari-
ans, teachers, all kinds of things, so I take issue with anyone who looks down on our front-line jobs. Many get
promoted to become area coaches, running anywhere
from five to seven restaurants and earning six-figure
salaries. Harvey Brownlee, our COO at KFC, started out
as an assistant restaurant manager at a Pizza Hut, which is
also where he met his wife, so don't tell me these are
dead-end jobs.

Turn Left First

We now have any number of programs in place to help us
go bonkers on our customer-mania message, such as the
aforementioned in-store BLAST program, which we teach
to all our front-line employees to help them deal with customer complaints. Also, since we've all been customers ourselves, it's really not that hard to figure out what makes them
happy. We call our in-store report card CHAMPS, which
stands for **C**leanliness, **H**ospitality, **A**ccuracy, **M**aintenance,
Product Quality, and **S**peed with Service. We achieve cus-

tomer mania when we deliver all these fundamentals with a positive, helpful attitude. We call it "100 percent CHAMPS with a Yes attitude."

One reason we lagged in our customer-satisfaction ratings is that many people in our company just didn't feel like that principle applied to them. It's obvious that the person who serves you your food needs to care about customer satisfaction, but what about the people in accounting or research and development or even our CFO? You could ask any of our people if they thought customer focus was a good idea and I'm sure they'd say yes, but I suspected many were also thinking to themselves, "Well, that's really part of someone else's job." And if that was the case, then how were we supposed to make customer mania a major company-wide initiative?

I got restaurant support center people at all levels focused on the idea of customer mania by asking every single person to come up with a list of ways in which they could serve our customer. One of our lawyers, for example, said he would be a customer maniac by making sure that our employees were treated fairly and equally in our restaurants. That would make the employees happier, and happier employees make for happier customers. Our CFO, Rick Carucci, said he would make sure that we invested in new equipment and services that would improve the customer's eating environment. My administrative assistant, Donna Hughes, said she would be more productive and also more money-conscious by watching her expenses and using fewer office supplies because if everyone in our company did that, then we would be more cost-efficient and able to offer a better value to our customers. As my assistant, Donna fields a number of calls from customers who have complaints. She vowed to do her best to direct those calls to someone who could actually help the customers with their issues.

All our "above-store" people now go through customer-mania training as well. Among the lessons we teach them is "turn left first," which means that whenever they walk into a restaurant, they should first turn left and go talk to customers, rather than turning right to go to the back of the store. This is a great way to make customers feel appreciated and to find out all sorts of information—how new products are being received, whether they feel like they're getting good value for their money, what they think we're doing right, and what they think we could do better.

Obviously, the customer is always going to be of the utmost importance to us, so we have to constantly reinforce the idea of customer mania. It's still something we struggle with, though we've definitely improved. Just the other day I ordered dinner at an A&W (from the drive-thru so they didn't know it was me), and it took ten minutes to get my hamburger and they forgot about my diet root beer. I went in to ask the restaurant manager what had happened, and he said that they had just gotten slammed that day with way more customers than usual. I know that happens sometimes, but at the same time, the customer doesn't care that you're having a bad day.

We've still got a long way to go, but we're committed to getting there. Achieving great service is not a challenge that's unique to us. I say this after just being told by Wendy that she was put on hold for twenty minutes before she could reconcile a cable bill. Yet, the Starbucks and Southwest Airlines of the world are showing it can be done, and we're not going to rest until we rank with them.

Customer mania isn't a program of the month for us, it's a program of the century.

19

Getting Things Done

Driving Results

I t may go without saying, but it's very hard to get all the parts of a company of our size and geographic diversity moving forward at the same time and in the same direction. And moving forward, of course, isn't optional. Companies are all about change—about driving change and then managing change. I like that Will Rogers quote, "Even if you're on the right track, you'll get run over if you just sit there."

To accelerate our push toward customer mania, I realized there was another very important thing our company needed to work on—execution. This was around 2003, and by this point, we had programs in place to help us achieve the goals we set for ourselves and to help us "walk the talk" when it came to our values. We had CHAMPS, customer mania, and our Dynasty Drivers. We had developed something called the Yum! Insight Marketing Model, which defines how to develop new products and what makes a good versus a bad ad. We'd institutionalized what works in just about every area of our business.

The building blocks were all there, but our results

were often inconsistent. And the reason is that our execution of these programs, which we'd worked so hard to develop over the years, was inconsistent. I've come to realize that one of the biggest gaps in business, as in life, is in the knowing versus the doing. We knew what to do, we just had to get better at getting it done. Customer mania and execution are now *the* major themes for our company.

Watch Out for "the Good Times"

In my leadership program, I talk about telling it like it is, for a very simple reason. If people don't first see things as they really are, then they'll never know what they're doing right and what they could be doing better. As I believe Napoleon said, "The responsibility of the leader is to define reality and create hope."

In 2003 we had plenty of good and bad news to share. We were now the leading global restaurant developer and had opened our eleven thousandth restaurant outside the United States. We'd reduced our debt by half, our stock had doubled, we had the best return on capital in the industry, and sales and profitability were at record levels. That was the good news.

At the same time, same-store sales growth in the United States and other countries had been on a roller coaster—up one year, down another. Taco Bell had lost its edginess, Pizza Hut's value ratings were slipping, and KFC was making promotional errors. (Here's one that really took the cake: KFC had developed a family promotion that featured a free cake, which was great until we ran out of cakes—on Mother's

Day!) What's more, while we had pockets of excellence in China, India, and Australia, our customers were still telling us that we were getting service right only about half the time in all our restaurants in most countries around the world.

I felt I knew that because our overall picture tended to trend upward, we risked settling for less than our full potential and getting away with it. As my father always used to say to me, "Potential means you haven't done it yet." And getting it done meant all kinds of growth for us.

It's easy to define reality when things are bad, but it's harder when things are good because people just aren't looking as hard for ways to make the business better. A former board member, Jamie Dimon, who spearheaded the turnaround at Bank One and is now at JPMorgan Chase, has shown me the power of defining reality by constantly comparing his company to best-in-class performance within the financial industry. We do this internally at Yum! by racking and stacking all our restaurants from top to bottom on key performance measures. Believe me, that drives healthy competition. Numbers don't lie and no one wants to be on the bottom for very long.

In addition to our internal tracking, our president of U.S. brand building, Emil Brolick, is a data hound, and he tracks progress (or lack thereof) by looking at the numbers and continually showing where we stand versus competition on key customer measures even when the sales and profits are booming.

When, for example, you present to your people something like those dismal customer-service ratings, which showed we had fallen behind McDonald's, Del Taco, and others, it makes a crystal clear, unarguable case that this is something they need to work on, even if business is good overall.

Sam Walton said, "The more you know, the more you care." What Mr. Sam realized is that imparting knowledge and information to his employees was a way of creating a sense of ownership and urgency around doing what needs to be done. So we try to let everyone know how we're doing at all times, just as much as you would know if you were the owner.

Keep Raising the Bar

Defining reality and communicating to everyone in our company where we were falling short was really just one side of the coin. The other side was that we had to make it clear to everyone that we believed we could do better. As Napoleon pointed out, you have to define reality *and* create hope.

To inspire our people to raise the stakes in our business, I brought in Larry Bossidy, coauthor of the bestselling book *Execution: The Discipline of Getting Things Done,* to talk to about two hundred of our top people. I introduced Larry by saying that the fact that his book happened to be called *Execution* wasn't the only thing that convinced me that Larry was one of the world's foremost experts on the subject. It was the fact that he had nine children and had told each of them that he would pay for their college education—up to four years, and that was it. And guess what? Every one of his kids graduated in four years. That's what I call driving execution.

In listening to Larry that day, I realized once again how essential it is to get the right people on the team when it comes to execution. There are some people who can get things done, and it seems there are others who just can't. That's why we move heaven and earth to retain our stars and the main reason we manage out our lowest performers—the bottom 10 percent at least—each year.

Declare War on Bigcompanyitis

One of the things we learned from Larry is that execution is a state of mind, a constant awareness that the bigger you get, the harder it is to get things done and that every manager at every level is in a daily battle to the death with bureaucracy, often just to keep it from getting any worse.

Jack Welch has said that when he was at GE, he hated—actively loathed—bureaucracy. In fact, I'll never forget how proud he was when he pulled his values card out of his wallet and showed me that they actually used the word *hate* in one of their company values—"We hate bureaucracy and all the nonsense that comes with it." When I visited Warren Buffett for the first time at Berkshire Hathaway in Omaha, I was shocked to discover that the total staff working in his home office was seventeen people, four of them part-time. If this I-hate-bureaucracy mind-set is good enough for Jack Welch and Warren Buffett, it is certainly good enough for me.

This natural tendency toward bureaucracy is often called "bigcompanyitis." Anything you can do to encourage execution is almost by definition discouraging bigcompanyitis. In general, my antidote to bigcompanyitis is shared knowledge and open communication, but I also think there are a number of specific things I do to drive execution.

Start Out Where You Want to End Up

Great execution starts with clarity of purpose and a clear vision of what you want to become or get done. As one of our franchisees once told me, "A road that leads to nowhere is hard to build." I wanted everyone in the company to know where we were headed and how we were going to get there. That's why I painted the vision for us to build the Yum! Dynasty, and articulated our key strategies for doing so in one page, our Yum! Dynasty Model.

Another example of creating a vision is what Sam Su, the president of our China division, has been able to accomplish. Sam is a multilingual Wharton Business School graduate and a brilliant leader. In 1989, when virtually no American company had successfully breached the business wall of China, he was given the challenge of establishing PepsiCo's American restaurant brands in a country that didn't even know what "fast food" was.

Sam started by recruiting the best people he could, but since there was very little tangible to show, he had to create a vision and sell them on the challenge. "We have the opportunity to build the most successful restaurant company in China," Sam told them. "And given that China is the biggest market in the world, we can be the most successful restaurant company in the world."

When the restaurants broke off from PepsiCo in 1997, Sam got his key leaders together, approximately fifty people, and used the opportunity to create a common vision every-one could rally around: "To build Yum! China into the most successful restaurant company in China as well as in the world!" The team came up with it together and adopted it unanimously.

"Once it was out there," Sam said, "it was just a matter of taking every opportunity to drive home this message at every level—at RGM conventions, in staff communications, in all internal publications, and so on. Now, when I say 'To build Yum! China . . .' the audience will finish off the rest. All our blue chips, strategies, and plans are based on whether they will help us get closer to this eventual goal."

Today, not only is Yum! the number one company in China, KFC is the most recognizable American brand name (not just bigger than McDonald's but also Coke, Pepsi, Nike, and Adidas), and the team is even more passionate about becoming the largest and best restaurant company in the world.

Execution begins with a vision and your people saying, "I understand it. I'm excited about it. I can help make it happen!"

Act Like an Entrepreneur

"Run this business as though you owned one restaurant." That advice came directly from one of our biggest franchisees and was later echoed on our visits to Home Depot, which had the mantra "Run each store like it's your only one." When it comes to execution, I think one of the advantages we have over most companies is our franchisees. We are essentially a giant company made up of small-business own-ers, although some of them aren't so small, and while we've locked horns with our franchisees on any number of occasions, they also help keep us focused on what's im-portant. Entrepreneurs are the absolute best at execution because their livelihoods directly depend on it.

Many of our top franchisees are totally self-made, and you can learn a lot just by observing how they treat cus-tomers and how they run their organizations. When I first got to Pizza Hut, I went to visit a franchisee in Fort Wayne, Indiana, by the name of Dick Freeland, who owned the highest-volume Pizza Huts in the country. We went to eat at one of his restaurants, and when we got there, there was a line of customers waiting for tables. He made a point of ensuring that we didn't sit down before all the customers had been seated first. When we were finally seated, the waitresses came up and kissed him on the cheek. Clearly, he put both his people and his customers ahead of himself, and you could just tell how well loved he was because of it.

Back at his office he had pictures of all his employees on the wall with his restaurant managers on top and his picture at the bottom—an inverted pyramid, which graph-ically demonstrated the importance he placed on restau-rant teams. I had to smile to myself. When I was at Pepsi, we had a huge internal initiative going on called Right Side Up, which at its core was that inverted pyramid. I re-member thinking how we had paid some high-priced consultant a ton of money to help come up with what Dick had figured out probably from just looking at a blank wall. It was a great initiative for Pepsi, but some people just know these things in their bones.

No New Programs of the Month

How many times have you seen a memo or an e-mail that institutes some new directive or policy or reporting procedure? How many times does that memo or e-mail also say, "The above directive replaces or rescinds the such-and-such policy or procedure"? Almost never. This harkens back to my duckies-and-goats philosophy about keeping it simple. Over time, these new policies, however small, add up, so you also have to be vigilant that the duckies and goats aren't nibbling your company to death.

Despite our best intentions, this is an ongoing battle. For instance, our area coaches, who are responsible for seven to eight restaurants, are in constant danger of being what I call "pencil-whipped," or so overwhelmed by paperwork and new programs created from on high that it reduces their ability to get things done.

Sometimes I think companies institute new programs of the month out of sheer boredom. There's also this kind of corporate time warp, where some new initiative is in the works for so long, by the time it's actually implemented, it seems like old news. So you end up coming up with something new even if what you've recently put in place is just starting to work.

I once heard a true story about the CEO of a major company who was so enamored with a new print ad campaign, he had the ads framed and hung them up in his office. The advertising lead time for some magazines can be months, but every day this CEO was coming into his office and staring at these ads up on his wall. One day he called in his advertising director and said, "Listen, I think this ad campaign is starting to get a little stale. It doesn't have the same pop as when we first launched it. I think we need to come up with something new."

"Actually," the advertising director said, "it hasn't even started to run yet."

Sometimes the worst thing that can happen to our company is me getting a free day in the office. I'm a creative guy and I can start dreaming up stuff to do when we haven't finished what we started.

When I gave a speech in 2003 about how we needed to get better at execution, I reminded everyone that we already had the formula for it in place: our Yum! Dynasty Model. We knew what our passion was, we'd already identified our formula for success, and we'd clearly articulated how we would win. We didn't need any new execution program, we just needed to get better at using the tools and executing processes we already had.

Avoid the Slow No's

Conflict is inevitable and productive conflict is essential. If people aren't pushing back, then you're doing something wrong.

Again, this is where franchisees can be very helpful. They *love* to push back. They have no stake in "telling David what he wants to hear," and fortunately, I have no choice other than to listen. I don't always agree with the franchisees, but there is no doubt they force me to more carefully consider every decision.

To minimize radio contact between ships at sea, the U.S. Navy has an expression, "Silence means consent." In business, just the opposite is often true; Silence means dissent. Have you ever been in a meeting where you sense there is obvious disagreement, but the disagreement never really gets put on the table? This is what I call the Slow No's.

A lot of people, when they make a proposal or a presentation, take a lack of criticism to mean that they have agreement. But there are people sitting there who aren't in agreement. They just aren't saying anything because it's no fun to tell someone no. Later, these same people will say, "But I never agreed to that," and the further along you are in the process, the more problematic this becomes. The Slow No's are the bane of execution.

If it's my meeting, I consider it my job to sniff out the Slow No's, to take the initiative and be very clear and ask: "Are you with me or not? Do you agree or disagree?" I've often said that if I'm in a meeting with five people, probably one person agrees with me, two are on the fence, and two can't wait to tell me how wrong I am. I'm going to hear from the last two whether I want to or not, but I need to flush out everyone else and get any conflicts into the open.

Some conflicts are simply territorial. For instance, I've rarely met a marketing person who wanted to raise prices, and I've rarely met a finance person who wanted to lower prices. So you have to take these prejudices into account when sniffing out conflict and making a decision.

Wipe Out "Not Invented Here"

And, for that matter, "I'm in charge here" and "This is the way we've always done it." It's the leader's job to create a culture that celebrates other people's ideas and achievements—the fact that if they win, you win. To my mind, this is a lot of what our emphasis on reward and recognition is about.

When I discuss this in my seminar, I use the example of my commitment, no matter what, to going forward with Crystal Pepsi. I was so convinced of my own wisdom, I failed to hear what anyone else had to say.

If you truly want people to wipe out Not Invented Here, then you have to reward them for doing it. We've started paying higher bonuses and telling the world about it when someone shares a best practice or adopts a best practice. For example, our KFC team in Australia has had more new-product innovations than anyone else. They've come up with boneless filets, chicken skewers, and a bundled meal called the Variety Big Box Meal. But they went one step further and did a great job of sharing their innovations with the rest of the company, so we gave them a bigger bonus. Then our U.K. team took those ideas and did a fantastic job implementing them in their stores, turning around their business as a result, so we gave them a special bonus, too. Larry Bossidy calls this "rewarding the doers," and we strive to do this as much as possible because people do what gets rewarded and follow the dollar signs.

Manage Two Up and Two Down

I always coach people to manage two up and two down for successful execution. You should manage two up because if you find out that your boss or even your boss's boss isn't on the same page you're on, all your hard work and effort could lead to disaster. When you lead your team in a direction only to have your efforts squashed because your superior never agreed on the objectives in the first place, your credibility suffers. I've seen this happen time and again when it can be so easily avoided by getting input up-front.

By the way, I think it's important to demonstrate the ability to think two up if you want to get promoted. Putting yourself in your boss's shoes forces you to think more broadly. I remember whenever I got the chance to meet with my boss's boss, I always told him (in a respectful manner, of course) what I'd be doing if I were in his place.

Managing two down is also critical if you really want to know what's going on and what people are thinking. For me, that means going to my direct reports and then talking to their direct reports and also visiting the front lines. This gives me the total picture of what's getting executed and what isn't.

In our people-evaluation process we have what we call "the 360s," which is feedback not just from your boss but also from your peers and the people who work for you. Obviously this can be very revealing. You learn pretty quickly who the real players are and who are the impediments to execution.

I also get 360-degree feedback from our top two hundred leaders. I learn how I'm doing and how they think I can do even better. Then I share what I've learned with the organization. For this to really work, I have to open myself up to criticism, but the result is trust.

If You Want to Make It Happen, Follow Up

One of the greatest failures to execute is the lack of follow-up. This seems so obvious, yet very few companies place as much emphasis on accountability as they do on figuring out what they want to get done.

Steve Reinemund, who was president of Pizza Hut when I was head of marketing there, is the best I've ever seen on this front. He always carried a three-by-five note card in his shirt pocket. When he saw something that needed to be done, he'd pull out the card and write it down. Like everyone else who witnessed this, I quickly realized that I had better write down the same things because he'd surely be on me until they got done. Steve got results everywhere he went, whether it was as president of Pizza Hut or Frito-Lay or chairman of PepsiCo, because he made a point of following up. People often lose track of what they've talked about in meetings or what they promised to do, but when you write it down, you won't forget it.

Get Better Today and Even Better Tomorrow

I love what Wal-Mart calls its "corrections-of-errors process." I learned that after every program, they bring the team together and ask what they did well and what they could do better. The goal is to run the same program again but to grow by correcting the errors they made the first time around.

When I visited Wal-Mart, I met their new chief human relations officer, who had come to them from another retailer. I asked him what the biggest difference was between the two companies, and he told me that at Wal-Mart they openly talked about their mistakes and how to improve on them. Feeling secure enough to talk about what you may have done wrong without risking your job was a part of the culture that didn't exist at the other place. As a result, people learned better, they followed through better, and their overall execution got a whole lot better.

It occurs to me that some of the companies we visited on our best-practice tour years ago have struggled recently. My hunch is that they have lost sight of some of the execution basics that got them to the top. I can't tell you how many times I've heard a CEO say after turning around a company that he did it by "getting back to basics."

Our goal is to get better and better at executing the basic building blocks of our business. It's the blocking and tackling that makes you win year after year.

20

Leaders Take Questions

Providing the CEO's Perspective

By now you can probably tell that I like *60 Minutes,* which is what I was watching when I saw Jack Welch talk about going bonkers on quality, giving me the idea for customer mania. I had another realization while watching *60 Minutes* a few years ago, when author Bob Woodward was being interviewed and quoted George W. Bush as saying, "I do not need to explain why I say things. That's the interesting thing about being the president. Maybe somebody needs to explain to me why they say something, but I don't feel like I owe anybody an explanation."

That's when I knew Bush was headed for trouble. With all due respect for the office, I completely disagree with him. In my view, it's the leader's responsibility to explain his or her actions every step of the way. And the higher up you are, the more important it is. But whenever Bush is at a press conference, he seems annoyed by the reporters who ask him hard questions. Unfortunately, it makes him seem like he doesn't feel much responsibility for answering to the people who elected him.

I consider it part of my job to field any question that comes my way; in fact, the tougher the question, the more important it is to answer it (unless it's about my private life). I even host a quarterly open call, where anyone in the company around the globe can call in and ask me anything they want to. I don't screen the questions beforehand or cut anyone off who might have a negative opinion about something. Anything about our business is fair game, and I think that's the way it should be.

Since I've been CEO, I've found that I'm often asked the same things over and over again, so I will address some of those questions in this chapter.

What do you think is the most important part of your job?

As CEO, I obviously have a lot of interests competing for my time. In fact, my schedule for the next two years is pretty much already set. I have five brands to think about, and our international business in 112 countries. There are also our board members, our investors, our customers, and so on. But the thing that I consider most important of all is our people.

I work hard to create a culture that will attract and retain top people because everything else follows from there. If we have great people working for us, then we can do a better job of making our customers happy. If we have great people working for us, then we can handle any problems that come our way. If we have great people, we can do just about anything.

One of my biggest challenges is setting priorities and then living up to those priorities. Because of all the time pressures I face, I could easily lose sight of what matters most, so I have to be ever vigilant about organizing my calendar around what I think is most important, which is first, our people; second, our customers; and third, profits. That's why, if you saw my calendar today, you'd notice that I present my leadership seminars to groups around the world several times a year; that every quarter I give a talk to our new hires to introduce them to our culture and values; that I do one-on-one coaching sessions twice a year with our general managers, about thirty in all; that I make our People Planning Process the most important process we have. You get the idea. If my calendar doesn't reflect what I think is most important, then I'm simply not doing my job.

How do you decide whom to hire?

When I hire someone, I try to get beneath the surface and go deep. The first question I ask is "Has this person demonstrated any leadership potential?" I ask for specifics and probe carefully to find out exactly what that person contributed. After all, success has many fathers.

I also look for enthusiasm, people who lean forward in their chairs, who get up on their haunches a little bit when they talk about what they've done. I like to see the passion and the excitement because that's what will allow someone to inspire others. The next thing I look for is an avid learner, someone who is curious, who has an ability to make connections, to pick up on trends, and to apply what's going on in the rest of the world to his or her business career. You obviously need smart people with a proven track record, but the real stars are passionate about what they do and are avid learners. Those two things make people continually raise the bar on performance.

The last thing I ask is "Would I want to work for this person? *Would I want my daughter to work for this person?*" If I can't get to that point, then I don't want to hire him. We want people who are what we call "smart with heart." We're very greedy about getting those types in our company. After the interview process, I follow up and check references by making the calls myself. It's easier to gloss over someone's faults with an HR person than it is with the CEO.

How do you build a winning team?

I think it takes a special talent for finding the right combination of people to make a great team. Putting the right people in a room together is one of those hard-to-explain phenomena that can really shake things up and get results. I like to call it "creating the super milk shake."

What I look for in teammates is a unity of values but a diversity of styles and experience. I don't want ten David Novak clones because what would be the point? I want people who will complement one another and build on one another's strengths. At the same time, they need to balance out one another's weaknesses so that just being together makes each person better than he would be on his own. This is tricky to pull off, and in order to do it well, you have to really know your people. I'm directly aware of the talent capabilities of at least two hundred people in our organization because almost all of them have attended my leadership program, which has allowed me to know them firsthand.

At the same time, you have to look for detractors among the group because one bad seed can be like a leak in the dam that leads to a major flood. The best thing you can do when you find someone like that is to fire him as quickly as possible. When we first started Yum!, we had someone pretty high up in the company who never really embraced our culture. One day, when our recognition band was playing in the hallway outside his office, he came out and yelled at them to knock off all the racket. I got rid of him before he sent the wrong signal to the rest of our people about what we considered important.

Firing someone can make a bold statement about what you care about. It's like the story David Ogilvy told about the cook who got fired for messing up the soufflés. The act actually had a positive impact on the rest of the kitchen because it sent a message that the chef didn't tolerate mediocrity.

Every time I've gone into a new job, I always looked for the person people wanted to have fired for good reason and then I'd do it. It's the surest way to say things are going to be better because there's a new sheriff in town.

You have to be careful that you're firing the right person, however, or you could end up making a huge mistake. When I first became president of KFC, even though there had been no sales growth for six years, I had the misconception that all the CFO, John Cahill, cared about was

making the profit plan. It seemed to me he was too ob-
sessed with cutting costs, which in some cases meant taking
things away from the consumer—like taking the bacon out
of the green beans—because it would save us *x* dollars. Almost every time he came up with a new idea, I'd say to
myself, "How is *that* going to make our customers happy?"

I thought John was so off base I told Wayne Calloway
I wanted to fire him. Wayne said he was surprised because he knew John was a smart and ambitious guy. I was
adamant about it until Wayne finally said, "Have you told
him how you feel yet? At least do that and see how he
responds."

The next morning I went to John and told him exactly what I thought. I said to him, "All CFOs can crunch
numbers and cut costs. The thing that's going to differentiate you from all the rest is if you can not only understand
the business, but figure out how to grow it. From now on,
every day that you come in, I want 'Mr. Growth' to be
stamped on your forehead."

You know what? He did a 180 after that. He took that
vision and ran with it, becoming customer focused, one of
my top performers, one of my best friends, and later on
CEO of Pepsi Bottling Group. Firing can be a good tool
for reinforcing what you want, but you also have to realize
that getting fired is one of the most traumatic experiences
anyone can go through—right after the death of a loved
one and divorce—and you have to conduct yourself ac-
cordingly. Everyone needs to know where he stands, no
surprises. Everyone deserves at least a chance to make
things better. And besides, people can surprise you.

How do you manage a winning team?

One of the most memorable things I learned from Larry Bossidy is that when you take the power of decision making away from people, you take the joy of the job away as well. The art of management is all about empowering people to make decisions while also coaching them to make the right ones.

I like to say that autonomy is an earned right, but at the same time, you have to know when to let go. It's like when I taught Ashley to ride a bike. For a long time she had training wheels, and I'd run along next to her to keep her steady. But eventually, as hard as it was for me, I had to take those training wheels off, stand back, and let her try it on her own.

By far, one of the toughest things to do when you get promoted is to manage peers who you know wanted your new job. The natural inclination is to be overly sensitive about giving them feedback. That's when you need to remember you got promoted for a reason. You got the job because you should have more skills to lead others, including your former peers, so be sure to give them direction like everyone else or you will soon create a vacuum for leadership that someone else will have to fill.

I focus on giving specific, real-time coaching so my teammates can benefit immediately. Larry Senn taught me a very effective tool that works in both individual and team settings. Start out by sharing "here's what you appreciate" about a person's work. By showing appreciation, you are setting the stage for acceptance of constructive suggestions.

Then offer suggestions by saying "and" you can be "even more effective" if you do such and such. "And" is a much better word than "but" because it's additive by building on a positive versus the usually negative "but" everyone is expecting to hear.

When a member of my team makes a presentation to others, we are at our best when we go around the room and each person shares what they "appreciate" about the work so far, and then we do the same thing for how it can be "even more effective." It's the best way I've ever seen to get the entire team's perspective in an inclusive, organized way. It also gives everyone an equal opportunity to weigh in. As the leader, I go last, so I get the advantage of the other vantage points and also don't bias the feedback because I have the most stripes.

Another method we practice is "team together/team apart." I pull the team together, get input from everyone, and together we make the best possible decision. Sometimes it's easy and there's total consensus, so the "team together" is a no-brainer to execute. When we don't have one hundred percent alignment, the head coach has to make the call based on all the input. We expect everyone on the team to support the decision even if they don't agree with the call, and that's what we mean by "team apart." The last thing you want is someone to leave the meeting and tell others they are not on board. Team together/team apart means you respect the final decision even if you would do something differently, and make it happen with positive energy.

A big concept I drive is having the attitude to work *with* people instead of having them work *for* you, being a "coach" instead of a "boss." Rather than tell people what to do, a leader helps team members figure it out for themselves. That way, when it's time for them to take the training wheels off, they'll have some experience to draw on. That's the way it was with me and Andy. When we were working together, I felt like I was making all the decisions even though he had the title. And when it came time for me to take over as CEO, I already felt like I'd been doing the job for years. He had the art of management down, and I didn't even know it.

How do you deal with your board of directors?

Warren Buffett once told me that the purpose of the board of directors is to ensure that you have at least a mediocre CEO. I treat my board like any boss I've ever had. It's my job to keep them well informed, full disclosure with no surprises. My golden rule when it comes to the board is "Share with them what you would want to know yourself."

I tell them the good, the bad, and the ugly (just like I've told you in this book), and if something comes up, I make sure they know about it immediately. When the AmeriServe crisis happened, we called our board members right away to give them the news instead of waiting for them to hear about it some other way.

I consider our board members to be a great sounding board, so when I'm selecting new ones, I look for people who understand and appreciate our culture and want to be a part of it, and for people with knowledge and expertise we can draw upon. We sought out Dave Dorman, the CEO of AT&T, because we didn't have anyone who was an ex- pert in technology and because 80 percent of Pizza Hut orders are phone orders, which he obviously knows something about. We also brought in Tom Ryan, the CEO of CVS, who started out as a pharmacist and knows the retail business from the ground up. The CEO of National Gypsum, Tom Nelson, brings with him knowledge of the construction-supply business, which is useful since we build a lot of new restaurants. We asked J. David Grissom, the chairman of his own private investment firm, Mayfair Capital, to come on board and chair our audit committee. We brought on Bonnie Hill, the president of B. Hill Enterprises, because she is a public affairs and governance expert. And we asked Jonathan Linen, the vice chairman of American Express, because about 10 percent of our business is paid for by credit cards.

I'm on the board of JPMorgan Chase, which I joined so I could learn more about the financial world and because I have tremendous respect for its CEO, Jamie Dimon. (I could never be on a board if I didn't respect the CEO.) A lot of people think it's a glamorous job, but it's not. It takes a lot of time, energy, and hard work. I always remember that when I'm dealing with my own board.

What do you do about the country's obesity problem?

Obesity is obviously a significant problem in this country. And because we are a huge restaurant company that actively markets its delicious food, good times, and family fun, when it comes to criticism, we are in the eye of the storm.

The real answer to the problem, of course, is balance—

exercise and eating sensibly. Nevertheless, this is an important national issue and we have responded by offering leaner, healthier options. We've introduced a Fit N' Delicious pizza at Pizza Hut. At KFC we offer salads and roasted chicken. Our Fresco Style menu at Taco Bell, which includes fifteen items with under ten grams of fat, is delicious. We continue to offer these products and are aggressively pursuing more choices.

We also constantly try to improve our food in ways that are nutritional and that will satisfy our customers. That's why KFC was a leader in removing trans fats from our cooking oils, a development that took two years of testing to make work without sacrificing taste. We also make nutritional information available to anyone who wants it, so people can make informed choices. And we're looking for ways to offer food with less sodium. Our main goal, however, is to offer convenient, great-tasting menu options at affordable prices, because, at the end of the day, that's the business we're in and that's what our customers tell us they want.

What's the deal with PETA?

You might have read that KFC has been a target of PETA (People for the Ethical Treatment of Animals) for quite some time. That's mainly because KFC is the most highly recognized chicken brand in the world. By targeting us, PETA makes the most news.

Chicken is one of the most popular foods in the world, so people love to eat it. Unfortunately, chickens have to be killed to make this a possibility. To be fair,

PETA is asking our suppliers to do this as humanely as possible, which is a good goal and we want the same thing. The primary thing PETA is pushing for is gas killing, and industry suppliers and their experts are not in agreement that this method is more humane. Until that issue is resolved, the PETA pressure will be on us and we will have to weather being unfairly singled out.

In truth, we don't own any chicken farms, chicken plants, or chickens. We get our chicken from the same suppliers that sell to grocery stores or any other place you may buy chicken. We ask our suppliers to process chickens consistent with industry standards and best practices. We also audit them to make sure it happens.

In Germany a few years ago, I was being interviewed at one of our new restaurants when a photographer, supposedly from a newspaper, asked me to pose for a picture. When I obliged, his "journalist" partner from PETA threw a bucket of red dye and white feathers at me. The picture of me covered from head to toe in "blood" and feathers was sent around the world. I know this kind of thing comes with the territory, but when I was getting out of my clothes, I felt my whole body shaking. The sense of personal violation was indescribable.

My family, including my parents and my sisters, have received threatening phone calls in the middle of the night. In the name of PETA I have received pictures of chickens scrawled over with red crayon (blood) calling me a murderer. I've had my church picketed while I was attending services. The same goes for other Yum! Brands executives. Believe me, I could go on and on.

I think PETA does itself a great disservice, and a particular disservice to the animal lovers who support them, by resorting to such abusive tactics. I'm aware of all sides of the issue and I happen to love animals, but big deal—who doesn't? But if PETA ever did have a point I haven't heard, the continuous attacks on me, my family, and our company make it harder and harder to believe they have something meaningful to say. And one thing is for sure, our company will never respond positively to corporate terrorism. Period.

What do you think about the reputation of CEOs?

I realize that a lot of people out there have a pretty negative view of CEOs, thanks to some high-profile abuses of power. But the truth is, almost every CEO I've ever met has been a good person. Generally speaking, you don't make it to the top by being a bad leader, and the vast majority of them have worked their way to the top the right way.

As with any other group of people in the public eye—think about athletes, politicians, or even men of the cloth—there are always going to be some bad apples. CEOs are no different. In my opinion, when a CEO gets into big trouble, it almost always boils down to hubris and greed. The good ones innately know the difference between right and wrong and make sure they have a competent and honest financial team so that greed isn't a factor. I have to sign off on all the financial reports, so I have to have a lot of confidence in my CFO, Rick Carucci, and I do. I also make sure everyone knows that no number is more important than doing the right thing.

CEO salaries are another big thing people talk about (although they usually don't ask me about it directly). I have to be honest and say that, yes, CEOs make a lot of money, but so do baseball players, even the ones who barely hit .200. I can't explain why our society values what it does, but I know that I make more than I ever thought I would. I also know that it's a job that takes an incredible toll. You're on call 24/7, you're responsible for hundreds of thousands of people, expectations are high, and there's tremendous turnover of CEOs who don't deliver. There's also a general recognition that a leader can make a real difference in driving shareholder value. Maybe that accounts for some of it.

I've also seen firsthand how quickly a CEO's reputation can change. When I first met Ken Lay at a Business Council meeting, he seemed like he was everyone's friend. But after the mess at Enron became public, he walked into the room one day and it was kind of like that scene from *Dangerous Liaisons* when everyone stops talking and stares at Glenn Close with disgust after she has publicly embarrassed herself. I'm not saying he didn't deserve it, but it was eerie.

Some CEOs get into trouble because they get so caught up in the trappings of power, they get out of the daily execution of the business, lose perspective, and forget to do their job. The antidote to that is staying grounded and remembering to be grateful for what you have every day. Thankfully, I have good people in my life who help me do that, and so do the CEOs I know.

How do you balance work and life?

Am I one of those guys who believes that if you're not working eighty hours a week, then you're not getting the job done? No, I'm not. I actually hate to work weekends, even though I often have to.

I used to think that I had to get up at five every morning and be at my desk by six. I still get up fairly early, around six, but I work out for an hour every morning, I read—often while exercising—and give myself some private time. I'll speak with my administrative assistant, Donna Hughes, who is an organizational genius, on the way into the office and go through the day, so by the time I get to the office at around eight-thirty or nine, I hit the ground running.

I also don't have meetings or phone calls set up every ten to fifteen minutes like clockwork—from 10:17 to 10:32 I'm doing this, from 10:32 to 10:41 I'm here, and so on. I'm not big on meetings in general because they create work for people, and the more people you have at a meeting, the more work you're creating. Meetings should be for taking a specific action and should have a defined outcome. I rarely have meetings just for updates, and I hope I've never had a cover-your-ass meeting.

In terms of both my workday and my life, what I try to achieve is balance. The hardest thing for me is the international travel and all the nights away from home. Work, for me, is tremendously rewarding, but the reward pays dividends in terms of personal time and time with my family. I try to spread the same message throughout our organization. I say, if your kid has a field hockey game, then go to it. (I used to take off to attend field hockey games myself when Ashley was younger.) The only thing I ask is that you tell your coach beforehand, and if you still have work to do, then come back to work afterward and do it.

Recently, I was out in Irvine, California, for Taco Bell's quarterly review, and Taco Bell's head of R&D, Warren Widicus, had to leave early to attend his daughter's volleyball game. When he got up to go I said, "Let's all give Warren a big hand, because he's got his priorities straight."

What are your thoughts on religion in the workplace?

I have debated whether or not to include anything about my religious beliefs in what is essentially a business book, but it is also my highly personal story, and my religious beliefs are part of who I am.

First and foremost, I want to say that for me that is what religion is—highly personal. I believe the same separation should exist between church and business as between church and state, although I would like to think that if we had one core value as a company, it would be "Do unto others as you would have them do unto you." I'm not one of those people who wakes up every morning and says, "God did this." I believe you have choices in your life.

I never attended church regularly until I moved to Louisville a little over a decade ago, and one of the main reasons is that I enjoy my minister and great friend Bob

Russell, whose sermons at Southeast Christian Church are very practical, very reality-based, with Bible lessons I can immediately apply in my own life.

One of the stories he likes to tell, along the lines of "God helps those who help themselves," is about a farmer who takes over a run-down farm in terrible shape and works his fingers to the bone in order to turn it around. One day, the minister comes out for a visit, looks around, and says, "God has done a wonderful job with this farm."

"Yeah?" the farmer says. "Well, you should have seen it before when God just had it by Himself."

As I said, every religion in the world is represented in our company, so I don't make it a practice to talk about my religious beliefs at work. But I do believe in God—and I do believe that He gives you gifts that you are supposed to do something with, that honors Him.

What keeps you up at night?

I take business matters as they come, so I sleep pretty well most nights. I suppose the things that make me toss and turn the most are the ones that I can't see coming, like the *E. coli* scare we had at Taco Bell. The only thing that comforts me then is knowing that we have the people and resources to see those things through over time.

The other thing I worry about is losing a real talent. I hate losing a great leader more than anything. I also hate it when I have to manage out a good person for poor performance or for simply doing something that is not in sync with our values. One of the hardest things I've ever had to do in my life—and I've had to do it more than once—is fire a friend.

Ron Daniel, the former head of McKinsey & Company, once told me that it was always the people who disappointed him that made business the toughest. I couldn't agree more. I've had people fall short of expectations over the years, but thankfully, they are in the small minority. Luckily for me, the good ones far outweigh the bad.

21

Unfinished Business

Learning Never Ends

Recently I was honored to be asked to be the grand marshal of the homecoming parade for my alma mater, the University of Missouri. Wendy and I led off the parade in a vintage Mustang convertible, and as we rode along, we waved to the crowd and threw candy to all the little kids who were lining the street. The problem was, I got a little too carried away with the candy and halfway through the parade route I ran out. So for the entire second half of the parade, we had all these disappointed little kids not getting any candy from us. Is there a moral to this story? Not really, although you'd think that someone who has been a CEO for a number of years would have a better understanding of the laws of supply and demand.

But this is what still gets me excited to get up and go to work each day. It's almost unfathomable how much I still have to learn. We've come a long way in ten years, but I feel like the greatest challenges lie ahead of us. Business is a journey to a destination you can never quite reach, and thank God for that, because always having another mountain to climb is what keeps you going.

There's an endless number of things I still want us to accomplish, so I'd like to use this chapter to talk about un-finished business—our hopes and dreams for the future.

Go for Greatness

Recently our top two hundred leaders gathered in Hawaii for a big conference that came about because we had hit one hundred dollars on a split-adjusted basis in our stock price—a big moment for us and a real measure of our suc-cess. It was as if we finally got to make up for that meeting in Keystone, Colorado, that I had to cancel during our first year because we weren't living up to financial expecta-tions . . . only better. It also happened to be the year of our tenth anniversary, but we weren't really there to talk about that. We started off with a Yum! cheer to remember Andy Pearson, but that was the only time we talked about the past.

Each of our presidents gave a talk about his area of the business, as did each of our country managers. They all came dressed to represent their local culture—Roger Eaton from Australia wore outback gear, Steve Pepper from Mexico was dressed like a mariachi, and so on—which added a bit of fun to the whole affair. I showed off some of the more unique recognition awards that people have come up with around the world, and everyone seemed to love seeing those. We had invited spouses and partners, and we encouraged them to participate in all our events because we wanted them, too, to feel invested in the success of the company. When I got back home, some of the best thank-you letters I received were not from my employees but from wives and husbands who were thrilled to have a chance to better understand what their significant others do all day long.

The point of this gathering, however, was not just to pat ourselves on the back; it was to look toward our future. We'd definitely come a long way, but there is still a long way to go, and the two things that were talked about again and again in terms of what we still need to work on were customer mania and execution. I made this point in my speech: "We may think we're doing great, but our customers still don't think we're great everywhere, and we'll never truly be great until they do."

Our way forward is not to come up with some new program to make this happen but, as I said earlier, to really get serious about doing a better job executing the programs we already have in place. We've already established that our Dynasty Drivers are our path to greatness, and now we needed to "go bonkers" on them. To close things out, I challenged everyone to go back home and develop a personal plan for bringing the Dynasty Drivers to life in their own piece of Yum! Brands. My job now is to hold everyone accountable for doing it.

Strive for Bold Goals

At the end of the company's first year I got about a hundred people together in a room to have our first future-strategy discussion. That's when we came up with what we called the "bold goals," which were very modest things like "to become one of the top ten companies in the world" and "to become *the* top restaurant company in the world."

The goals we talked about that day were so bold, they seemed unattainable to some of the people in the room. I believe in thinking big, but your goals also have to be based in reality. Otherwise, they're not goals at all but fantasies.

On the other hand, if you don't dream big, then what's the point of dreaming at all? Like I said, you never know what you're capable of. For example, since that "bold goals" meeting, *Fortune* magazine has picked us as one of the Best Companies for Minorities; *Hispanic* magazine as one of the Top 100 Companies for Hispanics; *Black Enterprise* as one of the Best Companies for Diversity; and *Fortune* again as one of Top Fifty Best Companies for Women. I'd still like to make *Fortune*'s list of the top ten best companies to work for in America, period, and I think we've got a shot. So much for unrealistic goals.

As for the future, I want to continue to dream big, even if from time to time people tell me I'm overreaching. If we set bold goals, then we at least have a shot at achieving them. If we don't, then what's the point of showing up tomorrow?

Pioneer the Wild, Wild East

Our business has grown so popular in China—we have more than three hundred Pizza Huts and two thousand KFCs there—one of the first phrases I learned in Chinese was "Duo-kai-yi-xie." That's what the customers would say when I walked in the door. It means "Build more."

I'm often asked how we developed such a great China business. As in most cases, it started at the top. Sam Su, who runs our business there, has led the way since 1986, building what is perhaps China's best consumer business today from from the ground up. He has assembled a top team of Chinese executives who have stayed together for more than ten years. Having locals run the business is key. Sending Americans into another country is like taking two years to find the bathroom. We own our own food-distribution company there and also have one of the largest real estate development teams of any retailers in the world, which has allowed us to expand into more than four hundred cities.

All this means we are on the ground floor of a booming category. I always compare it to forty years ago when such pioneers as Colonel Sanders, Glen Bell, Dan Carney of Pizza Hut, and Ray Kroc of McDonald's began building the quick-service-restaurant category from scratch. That's why I've challenged the team to build leading brands in every major food type that the Chinese customer likes. We are well on our way with KFC (which, by the way, has breakfast, fish, pork, and a delicious line of desserts called egg tarts) and Pizza Hut casual dining (which in addition to pizza offers escargot as an appetizer and a full line of pastas). I also said to them, if McDonald's can take America's favorite food and turn it into the largest chain in America, how do we do the same thing in China? Well, hamburgers are not that popular there, but Chinese food is, of course. So the team developed a new restaurant concept called "East Dawning," which offers a menu of local favorites. It's in its early days but looks like it could be a real winner.

We are often asked just how big we can get in China.

Well, we currently have 22,000 restaurants in the United States, which has a population of 300 million people. In China, we have only 2,300 restaurants in a country of 1.3 billion people. You can just imagine the possibilities. As I wrote in my 2005 annual report, one thing I'm sure of is that we'll have our ups and downs, but there's not a shred of doubt in my mind that one day we will have more restaurants in China than we have here at home.

As big as we are there, I am not a candidate for any special treatment, as I found out on a recent trip. When we landed the corporate jet in China, three inspectors got onto the plane to check us through customs. I handed one of them my passport, and I remember thinking at the time that it felt a little thin, but I didn't bother opening it up. Meanwhile, the inspector got a quizzical look on his face. He muttered something to me, which I obviously didn't understand, and then motioned for the other inspector to come over. They both looked at the passport. Then they looked at me. I had no idea what was going on until finally they gave me back the passport—and I saw my daughter's face staring back at me. I had brought Ashley's passport by mistake and left my own back in the office.

My first reaction was that it was no big deal, that Sam Su would get me in somehow because Sam can do anything. No such luck. Three hours later, I was still there and the customs inspectors were ready to call it a night. They couldn't let me go to the hotel, so I had to spend the night in this halfway house with a guard outside my room. I call it a house, but it felt more like a cell. I felt like the Man Without a Country.

The next day I did most of my business via conference

calls from my tiny room, which of course I could have done without leaving Louisville. Finally, the U.S. consulate worked things out for me, but I ended up spending a quarter of my entire China trip in a cubicle.

The next day, after leading a Yum! cheer at our China Restaurant Support Center, I told everyone there the story and that I was going to write a book someday about how you don't have to be that smart to be a CEO. Everyone roared with laughter.

The Rest of the World Is an Oyster, Too

Believe it or not, Yum! Restaurants International, which includes more than one hundred countries outside the United States and China, has opened up more than seven hundred new restaurants in seven years. And as in China, we believe we've gotten in on the ground floor.

Right now we have three markets that are huge growth opportunities for us—Russia, India, and continental Europe. In India—a country of 1.1 billion people—we are already the fastest-growing restaurant company, and Pizza Hut is the number one most trusted brand, with more than one hundred restaurants. We have also experienced early success with KFC, which even offers a vegetarian menu to appeal to about a third of the population. I can't tell you how passionate and committed our team members are. The Pizza Hut crews in each restaurant have created dance routines that they perform on the hour. Consumers are asked to ring the bell on their way out if they are happy, and the bells are always ringing.

As hard as it may be to believe, we are achieving the highest KFC volumes in the world in France. I guess the French just love to eat. And despite what you may hear about the French not liking the United States, that feeling sure doesn't translate to our food. We're also working hard to build the KFC brand in Holland and Germany.

Some of our biggest international news was made recently in Russia, where we formed a partnership with a man named Rostislav Ordovsky-Tanayevsky Blanco, who is the fast-food mogul of Moscow. He created Rostik's (named after himself, which is also what people call him), the number one chicken fast-food chain in Russia. He's very creative and known for bringing American restaurant concepts into Russia and adapting them to the local market. In addition to Rostik's, he owns a sushi restaurant, an Italian chain, and an American grill.

We wanted to make a deal with him to convert all his Rostik's stores to KFCs, but when I first met him, the deal was falling apart. We just couldn't get onto the same page.

He's smart and I could tell that he was feeling me out from the moment we first met in Moscow. We had plans to go to dinner the first evening, and Rostik said to me, "Well, we can get in the car, which will take an hour, or we can just take the subway, which will take about fifteen minutes." Security guards are assigned to me when I'm in Russia, and they immediately protested. But I knew Rostik was testing me. He wanted to find out if I thought I was too good to ride the subway. So I said, "Great, let's take the subway."

Rostik seemed to take special delight in schlepping this big group of security personnel and corporate guys on the subway, and he let down his defenses a bit after that. We hit it off over dinner, and at the end of the night I realized that in order to strike a deal with him, we were going to have to be as creative as he was.

I believe in following up and getting alignment immediately whenever possible, so after dinner, we stayed up until 1:30 A.M. talking about our issues. As a result, I challenged our team to come up with a partnership deal that got both of us what we wanted. We put a big chunk of money into his business in exchange for turning all his restaurants into Rostik's-KFCs and earning a franchisee fee on them. We also got the option to buy the company outright if we wanted to down the road. And Rostik got to keep his brand name, something he holds dear.

Just like that, with this one deal, we got one hundred restaurants overnight in a country with 140 million people. It took us ten years to open that many restaurants in China and ten years to do it in India.

Deliver the Bacon in the United States . . . Consistently

Our thriving international business contributes to a great portfolio. One of the reasons we can shoulder the ups and downs of business is that we have so many strong pieces in our pie. If one of our brands has a bad year, there are others that can compensate. If our U.S. business isn't doing as well, our international business can make up for it so that our overall picture remains strong.

At the same time, I hate that word *portfolio* because

whenever I hear it come out of my mouth I think it sounds like an excuse for our failures in some aspect of the business. In recent years, it's our U.S. business that has fallen behind the curve. The fact of the matter is, we've averaged only 2 percent profit growth in the United States in the past five years, and our goal has been at least 5 percent.

Frankly, nobody outside the company is expecting a lot of growth out of our U.S. business. Well, nobody expected our international and China businesses would be half our profits by now either, but today we are a truly global business. We're planning to surprise everyone with our progress in the United States, and we're working our tails off to make that happen. There are lots of doubters here because there's admittedly a lot to do, and I tell our U.S. teams, the rude reality is we haven't delivered yet.

Market Yum!

We've always heavily marketed our restaurant brands, but up until recently, very few people have known the name Yum! That's starting to change. In order to build employee pride in the company as well as investor awareness, we've started to slowly build our name and reputation.

In 2006 we were the first to sponsor the Kentucky Derby, which got us incredible press because no one had ever done it before. This was perhaps the last major sports event that hadn't yet had a corporate sponsor, so we broke through the clutter, generating millions of dollars of free publicity with the help of Amy Sherwood and our PR team.

We also sponsored the golfer J. B. Holmes, who has the

longest drives in the sport. No one knew him at the time, but he's from the University of Kentucky, and since we're in Louisville, I get to play golf with him sometimes. He's a good kid, so we decided to help him out. Right after we signed him, he went off to a tournament in Hawaii and did much better than we expected. He made the top ten, and he was hitting the ball longer than anyone had ever seen. Then he went to Phoenix and won the whole thing. The entire time, he was wearing a Yum! shirt with our logo on it. We got a whole lot of mileage out of that investment, and we were just trying to help the guy out. Funny how that happens. Sometimes you're luckier than you are good.

And, of course, we also have the job of attracting and retaining investors. Here, our biggest challenge is separating ourselves from the pack of typical U.S. restaurant companies like Wendy's and Jack-in-the-Box that only have one brand and don't have a significant international presence. That's why we continually reinforce the theme Yum! Brands is "Not Your Ordinary Restaurant Company," touting the fact that we have a portfolio of five brands, we have a truly global growth business (believe it or not, we now open up more new units outside the United States than any other retailer in the world, including Starbucks and McDonald's), and we have the highest return on invested capital in the industry.

You Need a Noble Cause

One of the jobs of the leader is to give employees a noble cause for their work. Just recently, at our monthly meeting of directors, I had the leader who runs our Pizza Hut and Taco Bell outlets in Iraq do a presentation. We have nineteen of them there, and he started out the meeting by reading a letter from a soldier who said that eating at our restaurants was like having a piece of home. That made everyone in the room feel just great about what we were doing.

We're always looking to find more ways to make our work meaningful. Recently we've gotten involved with a world-hunger campaign that will surpass anything we've ever done on a united global basis.

The challenge was to find a way to take Yum! to a higher level in giving back to the community, and our head of public affairs, Jonathan Blum, came up with this plan. His team did some research and found out that every four seconds somewhere in the world a child dies from hunger. The good news is that for a mere nineteen cents a day, you can provide enough food to keep a child from starving.

Yum! is partnering with the World Food Programme, an agency of the United Nations, to launch what we're calling World Hunger Relief Week. Our intent is for all the restaurants in our system to participate and raise money and build awareness of the problem. Our bold goal is to raise up to a thousand dollars per restaurant. (To kick it off, I'm donating 100 percent of my royalties from the sale of this book to the World Food Programme, so if you like it, tell your friends about it!)

Since we serve food to people around the world, this idea made perfect sense for us. But even better than that, since we have 35,000 restaurants in 112 countries, we could raise as much as $35 million, which would save the lives of 550,000 kids. I don't know about you, but I've never saved anyone's life before. If we can save one life, we'd feel great. But if we can help save half a million lives, well, that's about as noble as it gets.

The Work Is Always in Progress

Warren Buffett once told me about what he looks for in the companies he acquires. He said, "I'm looking to buy companies that are run by painters."

When I asked for an explanation, he said, "Most great artists have a hard time letting go of their paintings. That's because the joy is not in the finished work, the joy is in the painting. They are constantly adding a dab of color here, a little more texture there. I'm looking for the boss who is always tweaking his company, constantly trying to make it better. No matter how successful he may have already been, what he still sees is a masterpiece-in-progress."

That's the way I look at our company. It's a great place to work and it's getting better all the time, but there is plenty more to do. And besides, you never know what you're capable of.

AFTERWORD

I n the introduction to this book I talked about how my return visit to one of our stores in Washington, D.C., resulted in "You never know what you are capable of" becoming something of a mantra for me. My message here now is that "If it can happen to me, it can happen to you." I believe that you are only as good as you think you are, and that only you can hold you back, that positive thinking is self-fulfilling, and that you become what you think you can become. That in a nutshell is what will inspire you to know your stuff, give you real substance, and love what you do, which have always been the keys to greatness.

When I read business books or motivational books I find that if there is one thing I can take away with me, and, more important, if it is something that stays with me, then it is well worth the price of admission. Obviously, that "one thing" differs from person to person, but if there is anything I have said within these pages that helps you define your dreams and then go after them, then it is well worth the

effort it has taken to write this book and see it through pub-
lication. Whatever field you have chosen, whatever your aspirations may be, and however you choose to make them
come true, I hope one day you achieve more than you can
even imagine.

ACKNOWLEDGMENTS

In this book I talk about the importance of going from me to we. I'd like to thank all of you who made this book a gigantic WE project because of the support and lessons each of you have given me over my lifetime. This book could not have been written without you.

I know for certain I would not have been able to achieve what I've been able to achieve without the love of my wife and the first lady of Yum! Brands, Wendy. She has always challenged me to "go for it," from the beginning by asking me "When are you going to have enough guts to ask me out?" to the present by encouraging me to get over the anxiety of writing a book and "do it, David." Wendy is the most down-to-earth person I know, and she does her best to keep me that way. She has a heart of gold and courage beyond belief, fighting her juvenile diabetes without complaining and even risking her life and temporarily losing her eyesight in order to bring into the world our beautiful daughter, Ashley, who has unquestionably been the greatest joy in our life. Ashley, along with her husband, Jonathan Butler, now continuously show the power of giving to others, and it's clear they were made for each other, just like Wendy and me.

From the day I was born, my parents, Charles and Jean Novak, have given me a life of riches through their constant mentoring and encouragement. They have always been there for me, and I hope their Kansas Jayhawks finally get the NCAA basketball championship they've been cheering for. They have been almost as big a fan for the team as they have been for me and my loving sisters, Susan and Karen, both of whom I'm extremely proud.

I have also learned a great deal from Wendy's late father, Great Jack, and from her mother, Grand Ann, who happened to be much humbler than their family nicknames imply. Wendy's brothers, Jeff and Rick, are the brothers I never had, and her sisters, Cindy and Gretchen, have a special place in my heart.

When it comes to business, I've had the good fortune to be educated by the best. Andy Pearson, Yum!'s founding chairman and one of my best friends ever, was the most incredible teacher I have ever had; he taught me, among many things, how to stay young by being an avid learner. Roger Enrico encouraged me to think big, and I am truly thankful to him for having the vision to spin off PepsiCo's restaurants and the faith and confidence in me to be its leader. Of course my PepsiCo days started when Steve Reinemund took a chance on me by giving me my first chief marketing job, at Pizza Hut, and include Craig Weatherup giving me the opportunity to broaden my experience and prove I could do the job of chief operating officer at the Pepsi Cola Company. Both Steve and Craig showed me the value of seeing the potential in others. I also learned so much by listening to and observing Don Kendall, Wayne Calloway, Jack Welch, Larry Bossidy, Warren Buffett, Michael Jordan, Leo Kiely, Jeff Immelt, Phil Dusenberry, Brenda Barnes, John Cahill, Howard Schultz, Howard Davis, Norman Campbell, Bill Katz, Tom James, and Jim Walczy. Not to mention our past and current board of directors, who have had an immeasurable impact on both our company's and my personal growth: John Weinberg, Sidney Kohl, Jeanette Wagner, Ron Daniel, Jamie Dimon, Bob Ulrich, Massimo Ferragamo, Jackie Trujillo, Bob Holland, Ken Langone, Tom Ryan, J. David Grissom, Dave Dorman, Bonnie Hill, Jon Linen, and Tom Nelson.

Much of my education also comes from engaging subject-matter experts like Jim Collins on building great companies, Noel Tichy on leaders as teachers, Ken Blanchard on motivating the front line, Larry Senn on building culture, Patrick Lencioni on team building, Jack McAlinden on public speaking, Bob Rotella on the psychology of winning, Bob Russell on religion, and John Wooden on building sustainable success in business and life.

I owe thanks to all of our Partners' Council members over the years, some of whom are distinguished Yum! alums. Current: Graham Allan, Scott Bergren, Jonathan Blum, Emil Brolick, Harvey Brownlee, Anne Byerlein, Chris Campbell, Rick Carucci, Greg Creed, Gregg Dedrick, Roger Eaton, Peter Hearl, Melissa Lora, Micky Pant, Pat Murtha, Andrew Partridge, Steve Pepper, Rob Savage, and Sam Su. Alums: Pete Bassi, Cheryl Bachelder, Jerry Buss, Mark Cosby, Terry Davenport, Tom Davin, Steve Davis, David Deno, Aylwin Lewis, Robert Lowes, Tony Mastropaolo, Michael Miles, Bob Nilsen, Jeff Moody, Chuck Rawley, Michael Rawlings, and Peter Waller. Each of you has made valuable contributions to our business and to my learning curve from both the good and the challenging times we shared.

Special kudos go to our franchisees and especially to Pete Harman, Dick Freeland, Al Luihn, Allan Beebe, Francisco Rivera, Amghad El Mofti, and Arthur Ho for teaching me how to build the restaurant business the right way. The dedication of our one million team members serving our customers around the world inspires me day in and day out, and I have benefited so much by listening to and acting on what they have taught me.

Together, all these people have given me the education for my Taking People with You leadership program, and I'd particularly like to recognize Gregg Dedrick and Tim Galbraith for helping me develop the content and, along with Peter Hearl and Anne Byerlein, for all the days and nights away from home it took and continues to take to teach it around the world.

This book would not have been possible without my literary A-team of writers, John Boswell and Christa Bourg, and publisher, John Mahaney. John B. created the concept, structure, and captured my voice, Christa made it all work, and John M. made it better. All the conflict we had was indeed productive as we strove to do the best we could to bring my life story, learnings, and personality to life on the printed page. I would also like to thank John O'Neil, Jonathan Blum, and Chris Campbell for their editorial suggestions. And how could I fail to mention my assistant, Donna Hughes, who typed and retyped the manuscript what had to seem to her like a million times?

I am truly excited about Yum!'s Global Hunger Relief effort, which we are launching in conjunction with the release of this book, and I am gratified that all my proceeds from this book will go to help save the lives of hungry people around the world through the United Nations World Food Programme. Jim Morris, who led the the partnership from their end, is truly an inspiration.

Last but not least, I want to acknowledge all my friends for bringing me balance, perspective, and so many good times. I wish I could mention all of you by name, but if I've done my part over the years, you know who you are. All of you have given me an attitude of gratitude for the blessings you brought and continue to bring to my life, and I thank God for that every day.

INDEX

ABOUT THE AUTHORS

David Novak is chairman and CEO of Yum! Brands, Inc., the world's largest restaurant company, employing one million people and operating in 112 countries. He melded three underperforming companies (KFC, Taco Bell, and Pizza Hut), spun off from PepsiCo in 1997, into a unified international juggernaut, achieving at least 13 percent earnings per share growth during the past five years. He has been recognized as one of *Institutional Investor*'s top CEOs. He is the author of Taking People with You, a leadership program on how to build and align teams to get results. Prior to leading Yum! Brands, David was president at both KFC and Pizza Hut. He also held senior management positions at the Pepsi-Cola Company, including chief operating officer, and executive vice president of marketing and sales. He lives in Louisville, Kentucky, with his wife, Wendy. All of David's proceeds from the book will be donated to the United Nations World Food Programme in conjunction with Yum!'s global hunger relief efforts. He also serves as a director of the Friends of the World Food Programme.

John Boswell is a literary agent, a book packager, and the author or coauthor of seventeen books, including the #1 *New York Times* bestseller *What They Don't Teach You at Harvard Business School.* He lives in New York City.